The Art of Detachment

A Guide to Happiness in a Hyperconnected World.

Copyright Notice

Disclaimer

The information provided in this book, "The Art of Detachment: A Guide to Happiness in a Hyperconnected World," is intended for general informational purposes only.

While every effort has been made to ensure the accuracy and completeness of the information presented, the author and publisher assume no responsibility for errors or omissions, or for any results obtained from the use of the information contained in this book.

Readers are encouraged to exercise their own judgment and seek professional advice if needed.

Contents

Introduction 5

Chapter 1 8

Understanding Detachment 8

Chapter 2 15

Navigating the Hyperconnected World 15

Chapter 3 29

Cultivating Inner Peace 29

Chapter 4 56

Simplifying Life 56

Chapter 5 89

Detaching from External Validation 89

Chapter 6 120

Building Healthy Boundaries 120

Chapter 7 161

Embracing Change 161

Chapter 8 191

Mindful Productivity 191

Chapter 9 208

The Role of Gratitude 208

Chapter 10 229

Navigating Challenges 229

Chapter 11 258

Living a Detached and Fulfilling Life 258

Conclusion 284

Introduction

In a world buzzing with incessant connectivity and constant noise, the pursuit of happiness seems tangled in the web of our hyperconnected lives.

"The Art of Detachment: A Guide to Happiness in a Hyperconnected World" invites you on a transformative journey, unveiling the subtle yet profound art of reclaiming joy amidst the chaos.

In this book, we embark on an exploration of detachment not as an act of withdrawal, but as a powerful skill essential for finding serenity and fulfillment in a fast-paced, digitally-driven era.

Within these pages lies a roadmap to navigate the complexities of modern existence, where the incessant demands of technology, social expectations, and the rush of daily life often cloud our innate sense of contentment.

Through insightful anecdotes, practical exercises, and timeless wisdom, this guide offers a refreshing perspective on detachment—a practice that empowers, rather than disconnects, allowing us to thrive authentically in a world overflowing with stimuli.

We delve into the art of letting go—of attachments, expectations, and the relentless pursuit of perfection. By embracing detachment, we uncover the freedom to savor the present moment, cultivate genuine connections, and nurture our inner selves.

"The Art of Detachment" extends an invitation to reevaluate our relationship with the digital realm, guiding us to strike a harmonious balance between our online presence and the richness of our offline experiences.

It offers a blueprint to construct a life where detachment becomes an art form, enabling us to savor life's simplest joys, embrace uncertainty, and reclaim our autonomy in a world pulsating with information overload.

Chapter 1

Understanding Detachment

In the interconnection of human emotions and relationships, the concept of detachment emerges as a pivotal thread, weaving its way through the fabric of personal growth and well-being.

In this chapter, we will delve into the profound nuances of understanding detachment, exploring its definition, dispelling misconceptions, discussing the psychology that underlies it, and highlighting the manifold benefits it bestows upon personal well-being.

Detachment: What It Is and What It Isn't

Detachment is not synonymous with apathy or indifference, as some may mistakenly believe. Instead, it is the art of maintaining a healthy emotional distance, a delicate equilibrium that allows individuals to engage with life's experiences without becoming excessively entangled in their emotional complexities.

Detachment is the ability to observe and navigate life with a certain level of objectivity, without being overwhelmed by the emotional turbulence that may accompany various situations.

It's crucial to recognize that detachment doesn't imply a lack of care or concern. On the contrary, it is an acknowledgment of the impermanence of circumstances and the understanding that attaching oneself too strongly to outcomes can lead to unnecessary suffering.

By embracing detachment, individuals can free themselves from the shackles of excessive emotional investment, fostering resilience in the face of life's inevitable uncertainties.

The Psychology of Detachment

At its core, the psychology of detachment is deeply rooted in self-awareness and mindfulness.

It involves the cultivation of an internal sanctuary where individuals can observe their thoughts and emotions without being swept away by them.

By developing this mental space, individuals gain the capacity to respond to situations rather than react impulsively, fostering a sense of empowerment and control over their emotional responses.

Detachment also involves an acceptance of the present moment and an understanding that one's well-being is not solely dependent on external circumstances.

This mindset shift liberates individuals from the relentless pursuit of external validation and fosters a profound sense of internal fulfillment.

Benefits of Detachment in Personal Well-being

The rewards of practicing detachment extend far beyond the realm of emotional stability. By embracing detachment, individuals unlock a range of benefits that contribute to their overall well-being.

One notable advantage is the reduction of stress and anxiety levels. Detachment allows individuals to navigate challenges with a calm and collected demeanor, mitigating the negative impact of stress on both mental and physical health.

Moreover, detachment facilitates healthier relationships. By maintaining a balance between emotional involvement and detachment, individuals can foster genuine connections without succumbing to codependency.

This dynamic equilibrium empowers individuals to establish boundaries, communicate effectively, and contribute positively to their relationships.

Understanding detachment is akin to acquiring a masterful skill—one that enhances resilience, fosters emotional intelligence, and promotes personal well-being.

As we continue to explore the intricacies of this art, we embark on a journey toward a more balanced and fulfilling existence, where the ebb and flow of life are embraced with grace and wisdom.

Chapter 2

Navigating the Hyperconnected World

In the era of hyperconnectivity, the technological landscape has reshaped the very fabric of human interactions, giving rise to unprecedented opportunities and challenges.

This chapter explores the profound impact of technology on human connections, the intricate dynamics of social media in the context of relationships, and the crucial art of balancing virtual and real-life connections.

The Impact of Technology on Human Connections

Technology has significantly altered the landscape of human connections, both positively and negatively.

On the positive side, the advent of communication technologies has made it easier for individuals to connect across vast distances.

Social media platforms, instant messaging, and video calls have enabled people to maintain relationships despite geographical barriers.

This has fostered a sense of global interconnectedness, allowing individuals to share experiences and ideas in real-time, transcending physical limitations.

However, the pervasive use of technology has also had its drawbacks on human connections.

One of the most notable impacts is the rise of virtual interactions at the expense of face-to-face communication.

While technology facilitates quick and efficient communication, it often lacks the depth and nuance of in-person interactions.

The reliance on digital communication has led to a reduction in the quality of relationships, with people sometimes feeling more isolated despite being constantly connected online.

Moreover, the prevalence of social media has introduced new challenges to the dynamics of human connections.

The curated nature of online personas creates unrealistic expectations and contributes to a sense of social comparison, leading to feelings of inadequacy or loneliness.

The emphasis on likes, comments, and shares has shifted the focus from genuine connection to external validation, potentially affecting individuals' self-esteem and mental well-being.

Additionally, technology has changed the nature of communication itself. The brevity of text messages and the immediacy of digital communication leads to misunderstandings and misinterpretations.

Nuances conveyed through body language, tone of voice, and facial expressions are often lost in the digital realm, impacting the depth of human connections.

Balancing Virtual and Real-Life Connections

Balancing virtual and real-life connections is crucial in today's interconnected world, where technology plays a significant role in our daily lives.

Both virtual and real-life connections offer unique benefits, and striking a balance between the two is important for overall well-being and a fulfilling social experience. Here are some key reasons highlighting the importance of this balance:

1 **Real-Life Connections:** In-person interactions provide a deeper and more meaningful connection. Face-to-face communication helps build empathy, understanding, and emotional bonds.

2 **Virtual Connections:** Online interactions allow for broader social networks and enable people to connect across geographical boundaries, fostering diversity and inclusivity.

3 **Real-Life Connections:** Networking at events, conferences, and meetings can lead to valuable professional connections and opportunities. Building relationships in person can create a lasting impression.

4 **Virtual Connections:** Online platforms and social media provide avenues for professional networking, information sharing, and collaboration. Virtual connections can enhance visibility and access to a global professional community.

5 **Real-Life Connections:** Physical presence during challenging times can offer emotional support that virtual interactions may struggle to replicate. Human touch and non-verbal cues contribute to a sense of comfort.

6 **Virtual Connections:** Online communities and support groups provide a platform for sharing experiences, advice, and emotional support. They can be

particularly helpful when real-life connections are limited.

7 **Real-Life Connections:** Engaging in face-to-face activities and experiences contribute to personal growth, skill development, and cultural understanding.

8 **Virtual Connections:** Online learning platforms, webinars, and virtual communities offer opportunities for continuous learning and skill enhancement. Virtual connections can complement real-life experiences.

9 **Real-Life Connections:** Spending excessive time on virtual interactions may lead to neglecting real-life relationships and experiences. Balancing

time is essential for a well-rounded social life.

10 **Virtual Connections:** Leveraging technology for communication can be efficient, but it's important to avoid excessive screen time and prioritize in-person interactions when possible.

11 **Real-Life Connections:** Face-to-face interactions help combat feelings of loneliness and social isolation. Real-life connections provide a sense of community and belonging.

12 **Virtual Connections:** Online connections can be a lifeline for those who may face physical or geographical constraints. They can offer a sense of belonging and community in a digital space.

Balancing virtual and real-life connections is essential for maintaining meaningful relationships in the digital age. Here are several strategies to strike a healthy equilibrium between the online and offline aspects of human connections:

1 **Set Boundaries:** Establish clear boundaries for your online and offline interactions. Designate specific times for engaging in virtual communication and ensure there are periods where you focus on face-to-face interactions. This can help prevent the intrusion of digital distractions into real-life moments.

2 **Prioritize Face-to-Face Interactions:** While virtual communication is convenient, make a conscious effort to prioritize in-person meetings whenever possible.

Face-to-face interactions allow for richer communication, with the ability to pick up on non-verbal cues and build deeper connections.

3 **Limit Screen Time:** Actively manage your screen time to avoid excessive use of digital devices.

Set limits on social media, email, and messaging applications. Allocating specific time slots for online activities can help create a balance between the virtual and real world.

4 **Quality Over Quantity:** Focus on the quality of your connections rather than the quantity. Building strong relationships requires genuine engagement and meaningful conversations, whether they occur online or offline.

Invest time in nurturing a few close connections rather than spreading yourself too thin across numerous virtual acquaintances.

5 **Use Technology Mindfully:** Embrace technology mindfully by being aware of its impact on your relationships. Strive to use digital tools to enhance, not replace, real-life interactions.

Be present during face-to-face conversations, avoiding the temptation to constantly check your phone or engage in unrelated online activities.

6 **Plan Tech-Free Activities:** Designate specific times or activities where digital devices are not allowed. This could include family dinners, social gatherings, or outings with friends.

Engaging in tech-free activities promotes meaningful connections and allows everyone to be fully present in the moment.

7 **Reconnect with Hobbies:** Rediscover offline hobbies and activities that bring joy and fulfillment. Whether it's reading, sports, or creative pursuits, engaging in

real-life experiences can provide a break from the virtual world and contribute to a more balanced lifestyle.

8 **Regularly Assess and Adjust:** Periodically assess your online and offline interactions. Reflect on the quality of your relationships and whether adjustments are needed.
If you find yourself spending too much time in the digital realm, take steps to recalibrate and refocus on building real-life connections.

Chapter 3

Cultivating Inner Peace

In the relentless pace of modern life, where the discord of responsibilities, expectations, and external pressures often reigns supreme, the pursuit of inner peace often emerges as a beacon of solace and resilience.

Cultivating inner peace is not a passive endeavor but rather an intentional and transformative journey—one that invites individuals to navigate the complexities of their inner landscapes with mindfulness, emotional equilibrium, and the profound art of detachment.

At its essence, cultivating inner peace is a commitment to forging a sanctuary within oneself, a refuge where the storms of life may rage, but an unwavering calm prevails.

In this chapter, we will explore the multifaceted dimensions of cultivating inner peace, delving into the symbiotic relationship between mindfulness and detachment, unveiling practices that foster emotional balance, and discovering the transformative role of meditation in the pursuit of a serene state of being.

The Multifaceted Dimensions of Cultivating Inner Peace

Cultivating inner peace is a holistic process that involves various dimensions of one's life—physical, mental, emotional, and spiritual.

Achieving a state of inner peace requires intentional efforts and a commitment to practices that foster balance and harmony. Here are the multifaceted dimensions of cultivating inner peace:

1 **Mindful Awareness:** Developing the ability to be fully present in the moment without judgment is a key aspect of cultivating inner peace.

Mindfulness practices, such as mindful

breathing or mindful observation, help individuals stay grounded and focused on the present.

2 **Meditation:** Regular meditation practice is known to reduce stress, increase self-awareness, and promote a sense of calm. Meditation techniques, such as guided meditation or transcendental meditation, provide a space for introspection and inner peace.

3 **Self-Awareness:** Understanding and acknowledging one's emotions are fundamental to achieving inner peace. Emotional intelligence allows individuals to respond to situations with greater composure and resilience.

4 **Emotional Release:** Cultivating inner peace involves letting go of negative emotions and finding healthy ways to express and release them.

Practices like journaling, art, or talking to a trusted friend can aid in emotional processing.

5 **Healthy Lifestyle:** Adopting a balanced and healthy lifestyle, including regular exercise, proper nutrition, and sufficient sleep, contributes to overall well-being. Physical well-being is closely linked to mental and emotional states.

6 **Mind-Body Connection:** Practices such as yoga and Tai Chi focus on the integration of physical movement, breath, and mindfulness. These activities enhance the

mind-body connection, promoting relaxation and inner peace.

7 **Gratitude Practices:** Focusing on gratitude shifts one's perspective and bring attention to positive aspects of life. Regularly expressing gratitude through journaling or daily reflections contributes to a sense of inner peace.

8 **Optimism and Positivity:** Cultivating a positive mindset involves reframing negative thoughts and fostering optimism. Positive affirmations and visualizations are powerful tools in promoting inner peace.

9 **Mindful Spirituality:** For many, inner peace is deeply connected to spiritual beliefs and practices. Engaging

in activities that align with one's spiritual values, such as prayer or attending religious services, can provide a sense of purpose and tranquility.

10 **Nature Connection:** Spending time in nature and appreciating the beauty of the natural world can be a spiritually uplifting experience.

Nature has a calming effect on the mind and helps individuals reconnect with a larger, more profound perspective.

11 **Boundaries:** Establishing and maintaining healthy boundaries in relationships is crucial for inner peace. Learning to say no when necessary and prioritizing self-care contribute to a balanced and peaceful life.

12 **Empathy and Compassion:** Cultivating inner peace involves fostering empathy and compassion toward oneself and others. Understanding and accepting differences in others contribute to harmonious relationships.

Mindfulness and Detachment

Mindfulness and detachment are two intertwined concepts that play pivotal roles in the cultivation of inner peace.

These practices, often rooted in ancient philosophies and contemplative traditions, have found resonance in modern psychology and wellness approaches.

Understanding the dynamic interplay between mindfulness and detachment is key to navigating the complexities of the human experience.

Mindfulness: Present Awareness

Mindfulness is the practice of being fully present in the current moment, acknowledging and accepting one's thoughts, feelings, and bodily sensations without judgment.

It involves cultivating an acute awareness of the present, fostering a non-reactive and observant state of mind.

Key Components of Mindfulness

Several key components contribute to the essence of mindfulness:

1 **Present Moment Awareness:** Central to mindfulness is the cultivation of awareness in the present moment.

Instead of dwelling on the past or worrying about the future, mindfulness encourages individuals to focus on what is happening right now, whether it's sensations in the body, the breath, or the immediate environment.

2 **Non-Judgmental Observation:** Mindfulness involves observing thoughts, emotions, and sensations without attaching judgment.

Practitioners strive to view their experiences with a sense of curiosity and acceptance, recognizing that thoughts and feelings are temporary and do not necessarily define them.

3 **Intentional Attention:** Mindfulness requires intentional and purposeful attention.

Practitioners consciously direct their focus to a chosen anchor, such as the breath, bodily sensations, or a specific point of focus. This deliberate attention helps prevent the mind from wandering into automatic and often unhelpful thought patterns.

4 **Acceptance and Non-Attachment:** Mindfulness encourages acceptance of the present moment without a desire for it to be different. This doesn't imply resignation but rather a recognition of reality as it is.

Non-attachment involves letting go of the need to control or cling to specific outcomes, fostering a more balanced and peaceful approach to life.

5 **Cultivation of Compassion:** Mindfulness is not only about self-awareness but also about cultivating compassion, both for oneself and for others.

As individuals become more mindful, they often develop a greater sense of empathy and understanding, contributing to improved relationships and overall well-being.

6 **Open Awareness:** Mindfulness encourages an open and spacious awareness that allows for a broad and non-selective perception of one's

experience. Rather than getting entangled in specific details, practitioners aim to maintain a receptive and inclusive awareness.

7 **Mindful Listening and Communication:** Mindfulness extends to how individuals engage with others. Practicing mindful listening involves being fully present and attentive when others are speaking. Mindful communication emphasizes clear, non-reactive expression and thoughtful responses.

8 **Regular Practice:** Consistent and regular practice is fundamental to mindfulness. Whether through formal meditation sessions or informal practices, the ongoing cultivation of mindfulness helps

develop the skills and mindset necessary for maintaining present moment awareness.

Role of Mindfulness in Cultivating Inner Peace

Mindfulness plays a crucial role in cultivating inner peace by promoting self-awareness, enhancing emotional regulation, and fostering a deep connection with the present moment. Here's an exploration of the role of mindfulness in cultivating inner peace:

1 **Emotional Regulation:** Mindfulness practices, such as mindful breathing or body scan meditations, provide tools for individuals to regulate their emotions.

By bringing attention to the breath or bodily sensations, individuals can create a pause, allowing them to respond to emotions in a more measured and thoughtful way.

2 **Reducing Stress and Anxiety:** Mindfulness has been shown to reduce stress and anxiety by promoting relaxation and lowering the physiological and psychological impact of stressors. Mindful techniques, like progressive muscle relaxation or mindfulness-based stress reduction (MBSR), offer practical ways to manage stress and cultivate inner peace.

3 **Cultivating Gratitude:** Mindfulness practices often include gratitude

exercises, encouraging individuals to focus on the positive aspects of their lives.

This shift in attention towards gratitude contributes to a positive mindset, fostering a sense of contentment and inner peace.

4 **Enhanced Self-Awareness:** Mindfulness encourages self-reflection and self-awareness.

By paying attention to thoughts and emotions as they arise, individuals gain insights into their habitual patterns and reactions. This self-awareness is a key step in making conscious choices that lead to inner peace.

5 **Improved Concentration and Focus:** Regular mindfulness practice has been linked to improvements in concentration and attention.

By training the mind to stay focused on the present moment, individuals become less susceptible to distractions, contributing to a sense of inner calm and clarity.

6 **Acceptance and Letting Go:** Mindfulness encourages acceptance of the present moment, including one's thoughts and emotions. This acceptance does not imply resignation but rather a willingness to acknowledge and work with what is. Letting go of the need for control over every aspect of life contributes to a more

peaceful mindset.

7 **Mindful Action:** Mindfulness extends beyond formal meditation to everyday activities. Engaging in activities with full awareness, commonly referred to as "mindful living," allows individuals to bring mindfulness into their daily lives. This integration promotes a continuous sense of inner peace.

Synergy of Mindfulness and Detachment

The synergy of mindfulness and detachment is a powerful combination that lies at the heart of the art of detachment. The integration of these two practices creates a harmonious approach to navigating life's challenges.

Mindfulness serves as the foundation for detachment by bringing attention to the present moment.

When individuals are mindfully aware, they can observe their thoughts and emotions objectively, gaining insights into their habitual patterns of attachment.

This heightened awareness is essential for recognizing when attachment arises and understanding its impact on mental and emotional well-being.

By practicing mindfulness, individuals develop the capacity to respond to situations with clarity and discernment rather than reacting impulsively based on ingrained patterns.

Detachment, when coupled with mindfulness, becomes a conscious choice rather than a state of indifference.

Mindfulness provides the awareness needed to recognize attachments, and detachment offers the freedom to release them.

This art of detachment involves acknowledging the impermanence of life, accepting that change is inevitable, and embracing a more flexible and open-minded perspective.

The synergy between mindfulness and detachment allows individuals to approach life with a sense of ease, resilience, and adaptability.

Moreover, the combination of mindfulness and detachment contributes to emotional equilibrium.

Mindfulness enables individuals to experience emotions fully without being overwhelmed by them. Detachment, in this context, involves not letting these emotions dictate one's reactions or decisions.

By observing emotions with a non-attached mindset, individuals can respond to situations with a greater sense of calm and stability, fostering emotional well-being.

The art of detachment also involves letting go of the need for external validation and the attachment to specific outcomes.

Mindfulness helps individuals recognize the futility of seeking happiness solely through external circumstances. Detachment, in this sense, encourages a shift in focus from external achievements to internal contentment.

The combined practice of mindfulness and detachment cultivates a deep sense of inner peace, as individuals learn to find joy in the present moment rather than being dependent on future achievements or circumstances.

Practices for Cultivating Emotional Balance

Cultivating emotional balance is crucial for overall well-being and resilience in the face of life's challenges. Here are some practices that can help foster emotional balance:

1 **Mindfulness Meditation:** Mindfulness meditation involves paying attention to the present moment without judgment. It helps in developing awareness of emotions as they arise, promoting self-regulation.

2 **Emotion Regulation Techniques:** Learn to identify and label your emotions accurately. Understanding what you are feeling is the first step toward managing

those emotions effectively.

Practice deep breathing exercises, progressive muscle relaxation, or other relaxation techniques to calm the nervous system and reduce emotional intensity.

3 **Cognitive Restructuring:** Challenge and reframe negative thought patterns. Often, our emotions are influenced by our thoughts. By changing our perspective and adopting more positive or realistic thinking, we can influence our emotional responses.

4 **Gratitude Practices:** Cultivate a habit of expressing gratitude. Regularly acknowledging and appreciating the positive aspects of life can contribute to

a more balanced emotional state.

5 **Self-Compassion:** Treat yourself with kindness and understanding, especially during difficult times.

Practicing self-compassion involves acknowledging your struggles without judgment and offering yourself the same support you would to a friend.

6 **Social Connections:** Nurture healthy relationships and social connections. Share your feelings with trusted friends or family members. Connecting with others can provide emotional support and a sense of belonging.

7 **Physical Exercise:** Engage in regular physical activity. Exercise has been shown to have a positive impact on

mood by releasing endorphins and reducing stress hormones.

8 **Healthy Lifestyle Choices:** Ensure you are getting enough sleep, maintaining a balanced diet, and avoiding excessive alcohol or substance use. Physical well-being is closely linked to emotional well-being.

9 **Mind-Body Practices:** Explore mind-body practices such as yoga or tai chi. These activities combine physical movement with mindfulness and can help integrate the mind and body for improved emotional balance.

10 **Set Realistic Goals:** Break down larger tasks into smaller, manageable goals. Setting realistic expectations for yourself

can prevent feelings of overwhelm and frustration.

11 **Seek Professional Support:** If needed, don't hesitate to seek help from mental health professionals. Therapy can provide valuable tools and insights to help manage and understand emotions.

12 **Reflective Practices:** Take time for self-reflection. Journaling or introspective practices can help you gain insight into your emotions and thought patterns.

Chapter 4

Simplifying Life

In a world marked by constant demands, rapid changes, and an abundance of information, the pursuit of a simpler and more meaningful life has become a compelling journey for many.

This chapter, aptly titled "Simplifying Life," invites readers to embark on a transformative exploration of the principles, practices, and mindset shifts that can lead to a more streamlined and fulfilling existence.

As we navigate the complexities of modern life, the need to simplify becomes increasingly evident.

A Fast-Paced Society

A fast-paced society refers to a social environment characterized by rapid and accelerated activities, lifestyles, and technological advancements.

In such a society, individuals and communities experience a heightened pace of life, where changes, information, and activities unfold swiftly.

Several key elements contribute to the characterization of a fast-paced society:

1 **Rapid Technological Advancements:** In a fast-paced society, technology evolves quickly, leading to constant innovation and the rapid adoption of new tools,

devices, and communication platforms. This technological acceleration influences various aspects of daily life, from work practices to personal interactions.

2 **Quick Decision-Making and Information Processing:** Individuals in a fast-paced society often find themselves making decisions swiftly and processing information rapidly.

The need for quick responses is driven by the abundance of information and the demands of an environment that prioritizes efficiency.

3 **Accelerated Work Environments:** Workplaces in a fast-paced society are characterized by high demands, tight deadlines, and a constant pressure to

increase productivity.

The business world often adapts to a competitive and dynamic landscape, requiring employees to work efficiently and meet quick turnaround times.

4 **Instant Communication and Connectivity:** Communication in a fast-paced society occurs instantly, facilitated by the widespread use of smartphones, social media, and other digital platforms. Individuals can connect with each other, access information, and share updates in real-time, contributing to an environment of constant connectivity.

5 **Quick Consumer Trends and Product Lifecycles:** Consumer preferences and trends change rapidly in a fast-paced

society.

Industries such as fashion, technology, and entertainment experience quick turnovers in product lifecycles. This leads to a culture of continuous consumption and the constant pursuit of the latest trends.

6 **High Mobility and Globalization:** People in fast-paced societies often experience high levels of mobility.

Globalization and advancements in transportation make it easier for individuals to travel, conduct business internationally, and experience a more interconnected world.

7 **Increased Expectations for Multitasking:** Multitasking becomes a common

expectation in a fast-paced society. Individuals are often required to handle multiple tasks simultaneously, whether at work, in education, or in personal life, contributing to a culture of constant activity.

8 **24/7 Accessibility and Availability:** The boundary between work and personal life may blur in a fast-paced society, as individuals are expected to be accessible and available around the clock.

The advent of remote work and global communication further contributes to this constant availability.

9 **Shortened Attention Spans:** With the abundance of information and stimuli, individuals in fast-paced societies may

experience shortened attention spans. This can affect how people consume information, engage with content, and make decisions.

10 **Pressure for Continuous Improvement:** The fast-paced nature of society creates an environment where continuous improvement and adaptation are essential.

Individuals and organizations must be agile and responsive to stay competitive and relevant in rapidly changing circumstances.

Challenges of a Fast-Paced Society

In a fast-paced society, the art of detachment faces numerous challenges that can make it difficult for individuals to maintain a sense of balance and inner peace. Here are some key challenges posed by a fast-paced lifestyle in relation to detachment:

1 **Constant Distractions:** The fast-paced nature of modern life is often characterized by a barrage of stimuli, including notifications, emails, and social media updates.

These constant distractions make it challenging for individuals to cultivate mindfulness and detach from the stream of information, as the mind is constantly pulled in various directions.

2 **Pressure for Instant Results:** In a society that values efficiency and immediate

results, there is often a heightened sense of urgency.

The pressure to achieve instant success or rapid progress in various aspects of life can lead to heightened attachment to outcomes. Detaching from the need for quick results becomes a significant challenge in such an environment.

3 **Overwhelm and Stress:** The fast pace of daily life can contribute to feelings of overwhelm and stress.

When individuals are constantly juggling multiple responsibilities and deadlines, the emotional and mental toll can make it difficult to step back and detach from the intensity of the moment. The urgency of tasks may overshadow the need for mindful contemplation.

4 **Social Comparison and Competition:** Social media and the pervasive culture of comparison in a fast-paced society can intensify attachment to external validation and success.

The constant exposure to others' achievements can create a sense of competition and the fear of falling behind, making detachment from societal expectations and standards a formidable challenge.

5 **Lack of Time for Self-Reflection:** The hustle and bustle of a fast-paced lifestyle often leave little time for self-reflection. Detachment requires moments of introspection and self-awareness, which

may be neglected in a society that prioritizes constant productivity and external achievements.

The scarcity of time for reflection can hinder the development of a detached perspective.

6 **Cultural Emphasis on Busyness:** Some societies place a high value on busyness as a status symbol, equating a hectic schedule with success and importance.

This cultural emphasis on constant activity can foster a mindset of perpetual motion, leaving little room for the intentional slowing down and detachment necessary for a more mindful and balanced life.

7 **Technological Overload:** The prevalence of technology in a fast-paced society can contribute to information overload and a constant sense of connectivity.

This digital saturation can make it challenging for individuals to detach from the virtual world and find moments of solitude and quiet reflection.

Minimalism: Less Stuff, More Happiness

Minimalism is a lifestyle philosophy that advocates for simplifying one's life by focusing on essential aspects and decluttering unnecessary possessions.

The core principle of minimalism is often summarized by the phrase "less stuff, more happiness." This concept has gained popularity in response to the consumer-driven culture that encourages the accumulation of material possessions.

Here are some key aspects of minimalism and how they contribute to a potentially happier and more fulfilling life:

1 **Simplicity and Clarity:** Minimalism encourages individuals to pare down their belongings to the essentials.

By reducing physical clutter, people often experience a clearer and more focused mindset. This simplicity can extend beyond physical objects to other aspects of life, such as simplifying daily routines, work tasks, and social commitments.

2 **Intentional Living:** Minimalism emphasizes intentional living, where individuals make deliberate choices about the things they bring into their lives.

This involves being mindful of purchases, relationships, and activities. By aligning actions with personal values and priorities, we find a greater sense of purpose and fulfillment.

3 **Financial Freedom:** The pursuit of minimalism often involves cutting unnecessary expenses and avoiding consumerism.

This can lead to financial freedom as individuals focus on spending money on experiences or items that truly add value to their lives. The reduced financial burden can contribute to a sense of security and peace of mind.

4 **Reduced Stress and Overwhelm:** Living in a cluttered environment or managing an excess of possessions can contribute to stress and overwhelm.

Minimalism promotes the idea that a simplified living space can lead to a more peaceful and serene lifestyle. This, in turn, may improve mental well-being and reduce stress levels.

5 **Mindful Consumption:** Minimalism encourages a shift from mindless consumption to mindful consumption. Rather than acquiring items for the sake of owning more, individuals are prompted to consider the true value and

utility of each possession. This shift can lead to a more sustainable and environmentally friendly lifestyle.

6 **Increased Time and Energy:** With fewer possessions to manage and fewer commitments to juggle, minimalism can free up time and energy for pursuits that bring genuine joy and satisfaction.

This may include spending more time with loved ones, pursuing hobbies, or engaging in personal development activities.

It's important to note that minimalism is a highly individualistic concept, and its interpretation can vary from person to person. While some may find joy and contentment in a minimalist lifestyle, it may not be suitable for everyone. The key is to find a balance that aligns with one's values and enhances overall well-being.

Here are some steps to help you transition to a minimalist lifestyle:

1 **Define Your Values:** Before embarking on a minimalist journey, reflect on your core values and priorities. Identify what truly brings you joy and fulfillment, and use this understanding as a guide for simplifying your life.

2 **Declutter Your Physical Space:** Start by decluttering your living space. Go through your belongings and identify items that no longer serve a purpose or bring you happiness.

Donate, sell, or recycle these items, keeping only what adds value to your life. This process can be gradual, focusing on one area at a time.

3 **Streamline Your Wardrobe:** Adopt a minimalist approach to your wardrobe by curating a collection of versatile, high-quality clothing items. Consider the concept of a capsule wardrobe, where you have a limited number of essential pieces that can be mixed and matched easily.

4 **Digital Decluttering:** Extend your decluttering efforts to your digital life. Organize your computer files, delete unnecessary apps, and clean up your email inbox. A streamlined digital

environment can contribute significantly to a more focused and simplified life.

5 **Mindful Consumption:** Cultivate a habit of mindful consumption. Before making a purchase, ask yourself whether the item is truly necessary and aligns with your values. Avoid impulse buying and focus on acquiring possessions that enhance your life rather than burden it.

6 **Prioritize Experiences Over Possessions:** Shift your focus from accumulating possessions to collecting experiences. Invest your time and resources in activities, relationships, and adventures that bring lasting joy and fulfillment.

7 **Create Routines and Habits:** Establish simple and intentional routines in your

daily life. Develop habits that promote well-being, such as regular exercise, mindfulness practices, and adequate sleep. Routines can create a sense of stability and simplicity.

8 **Set Boundaries:** Learn to say no to commitments, possessions, or activities that don't align with your values or contribute positively to your life. Setting boundaries allows you to focus on what truly matters to you.

9 **Embrace Minimalist Design:** Consider incorporating minimalist design principles into your living space. Opt for clean lines, open spaces, and a limited color palette. A visually clutter-free environment can have a positive impact on your mental

well-being.

10 **Practice Gratitude:** Cultivate a mindset of gratitude for what you have. Regularly express appreciation for the simple pleasures in your life, fostering contentment and reducing the desire for excess.

Streamlining Your Digital Life

Streamlining your digital life, as part of "the art of detaching," involves minimizing digital clutter, reducing distractions, and fostering a healthier relationship with technology. Here are some key principles and strategies to achieve a more mindful and intentional approach to your digital existence:

1 **Digital Decluttering:** Similar to decluttering physical spaces, digital decluttering involves organizing and minimizing your digital footprint.

   This includes cleaning up your email inbox, organizing files and folders, and deleting unnecessary apps and files. A streamlined digital space can contribute to improved focus and productivity.

2 **Mindful Social Media Use:** Social media can be a significant source of digital overwhelm. Consider detoxing your social media accounts by unfollowing accounts that do not add value or contribute to your well-being.

   Set specific time limits for social media use to avoid mindless scrolling, and be intentional about the content you consume.

3 **Digital Detox Periods:** Introduce regular periods of digital detox where you disconnect from technology. This could be a few hours each day, a day per week, or longer breaks during holidays.

Use this time to engage in activities that don't involve screens, such as reading, spending time outdoors, or connecting with friends and family face-to-face.

4 **Prioritize Notifications:** Reduce digital distractions by carefully selecting which notifications you allow. Turn off non-essential notifications to minimize interruptions and regain control over your attention.

Consider setting specific times during the day to check messages and emails, rather than being constantly reactive to incoming notifications.

5 **Digital Minimalism in Apps and Devices:** Apply principles of digital minimalism by uninstalling or disabling apps that don't serve a purpose or add value to your life. Consider using tools that help you track and manage screen time to become more aware of your digital habits. Also, evaluate your device usage and consider simplifying your tech ecosystem.

6 **Simplify Digital Relationships:** Review your digital connections and consider whether your online relationships are adding value to your life.

Unsubscribe from newsletters that no longer interest you, clean up your contacts, and assess online groups and communities. Quality over quantity can apply to your digital connections as well.

7 **Digital Well-Being Features:** Many devices and apps now offer digital well-being features that help you understand and manage your screen time.

Take advantage of these tools to set limits, track usage patterns, and receive reminders to take breaks. This can contribute to a healthier and more mindful use of technology.

8 **Create a Digital Mindfulness Routine:** Incorporate mindfulness practices into your digital routine. This can include

activities such as meditation, deep breathing exercises, or simply taking a moment to be present before engaging with your devices.

These practices can help you detach from the constant stream of information and maintain a more balanced relationship with technology.

The Freedom of Letting Go

The freedom of letting go encapsulates a transformative approach to life, emphasizing the liberation that comes from releasing attachments, expectations, and the need for control.

It involves cultivating a mindset that allows individuals to surrender to the natural ebb and flow of existence, finding empowerment in the act of letting go rather than holding on tightly.

The essence of this freedom lies in embracing impermanence and acknowledging that, by relinquishing the grip on the past, worries about the future, and fixed notions, one can open the door to a more liberated and authentic way of living.

In the freedom of letting go, individuals discover a profound sense of inner peace and resilience.

It involves relinquishing the burdens of regret, resentment, and the constant pursuit of perfection, paving the way for a lighter, more joyful existence. This transformative process encourages a mindful presence in the current moment, fostering a genuine acceptance of oneself and others.

As individuals embark on the journey of letting go, they find liberation from the constraints of rigid expectations, allowing for personal growth, deeper connections, and an enriched experience of life's unfolding journey.

The freedom of letting go becomes a pathway to a more harmonious and fulfilling way of being, offering the space to flourish unencumbered by the weight of unnecessary baggage.

Here are steps to help you navigate this process:

1 **Reflect on Your Values:** Identify and clarify your core values. Understand what truly matters to you and what you want to prioritize in your life.

2 **Assess Your Possessions:** Evaluate your belongings and declutter. Keep only the items that serve a purpose or bring you joy. Consider adopting a minimalist mindset to simplify your material possessions.

3 **Embrace Minimalism:** Adopt a minimalist lifestyle, focusing on quality over quantity. Reduce unnecessary purchases and learn to appreciate the value of experiences and relationships over material possessions.

4 **Manage Your Finances:** Simplify your financial life by creating a budget, cutting unnecessary expenses, and avoiding debt. Save and invest wisely to secure your financial future.

5 **Let Go of Toxic Relationships:** Assess your relationships and let go of toxic ones. Surround yourself with people who support your well-being and share your values.

6 **Practice Mindfulness and Meditation:** Cultivate mindfulness to stay present and focused on the current moment. Meditation can help you detach from unnecessary worries and stressors.

7 **Set Boundaries:** Learn to say no when necessary. Establish clear boundaries to

protect your time and energy. This includes setting limits on work, social obligations, and other commitments.

8 **Simplify Your Schedule:** Streamline your daily activities and commitments. Prioritize tasks that align with your values and bring fulfillment. Avoid overloading your schedule with unnecessary obligations.

9 **Disconnect from Technology:** Limit your use of technology and social media. Detaching from constant notifications and updates can contribute to a more peaceful and focused life.

10 **Cultivate Gratitude:** Focus on gratitude for what you have rather than dwelling on what you lack. This mindset shift can

lead to a more content and fulfilled life.

11 **Accept Impermanence:** Understand that change is a natural part of life. Embrace impermanence, and let go of attachments to outcomes and material possessions.

12 **Simplify Your Goals:** Set realistic and meaningful goals. Simplify your ambitions to align with your values, reducing unnecessary stress and pressure.

13 **Focus on Personal Growth:** Invest time and energy in self-improvement and personal growth. This can lead to a more fulfilling and purposeful life.

14 **Enjoy Nature:** Spend time in nature to appreciate its simplicity and beauty. Connecting with the natural world can

bring a sense of peace and perspective.

Chapter 5

Detaching from External Validation

Detaching from external validation is a transformative journey that involves breaking free from the shackles of seeking approval and recognition from others.

In a world often driven by external expectations, individuals find themselves constantly striving to meet societal standards or seeking validation through the opinions of others.

However, true personal growth and fulfillment come when one learns to rely on internal validation, finding worth and purpose within oneself rather than constantly seeking affirmation from external sources.

Embracing self-validation requires a shift in mindset, fostering a deep sense of self-awareness and confidence. It involves recognizing that one's worth is not solely determined by external accolades or the approval of others but is inherently rooted in one's unique qualities, values, and experiences.

Detaching from external validation empowers individuals to cultivate a strong sense of self-esteem and authenticity, fostering resilience in the face of societal expectations.

This liberation allows for more genuine connections with others, as relationships become grounded in authenticity rather than the pursuit of validation.

Ultimately, the journey towards detaching from external validation is a powerful step towards self-discovery and personal fulfillment.

Breaking Free from Social Expectations

Breaking free from social expectations is essential for personal growth, authenticity, and overall well-being.

Societal norms and expectations often shape individuals' behaviors, choices, and aspirations. While some conformity is necessary for social cohesion, it is equally crucial for individuals to assert their autonomy and break free from rigid expectations.

Here are key reasons highlighting the importance of breaking free from social expectations:

1 **Authenticity and Self-Discovery:** Embracing one's true self requires breaking free from societal molds. Social expectations limit self-expression and authenticity, hindering the process of self-discovery.

Social expectations often prescribe certain norms and behaviors, discouraging deviation from established standards. This constraint can hinder self-expression and authenticity, impeding the process of self-discovery.

Fear of judgment or nonconformity may lead individuals to suppress genuine feelings and adopt socially acceptable personas, limiting their ability to explore and understand their true selves.

Embracing authenticity becomes challenging when conformity to societal expectations takes precedence over personal exploration and expression.

By defying these expectations, you become free to explore and understand your values, passions, and unique identity.

2 **Personal Fulfillment:** Conforming to societal expectations at the expense of personal desires can lead to a sense of emptiness and unfulfillment.

When individuals prioritize societal norms over their authentic aspirations, they may sacrifice their true selves. This leads to a disconnection from personal passions and a suppression of individuality, leaving a void within.

The absence of genuine fulfillment arises from living a life that aligns with external expectations but neglects the inner yearnings and authentic desires that bring true joy and purpose.

However, pursuing one's authentic goals and passions, even if they deviate from societal norms, fosters a deeper sense of purpose and satisfaction.

3 **Resilience and Adaptability:** Breaking free from rigid social expectations cultivates resilience and adaptability.

In a rapidly changing world, individuals who can navigate uncertainties and adapt to evolving circumstances often thrive. The ability to forge one's path fosters resilience and a capacity to confront challenges with a more open and innovative mindset.

4 **Mental Health and Well-Being:** Constantly striving to meet societal expectations can contribute to stress, anxiety, and feelings of inadequacy.

The relentless pursuit of external

standards often creates an unrealistic burden, fostering a sense of not measuring up. This societal pressure can erode self-esteem and mental well-being, as individuals feel compelled to meet often unattainable benchmarks, resulting in chronic stress and heightened anxiety about perceived inadequacies.

Prioritizing mental health requires individuals to set boundaries, establish their own standards, and reject unrealistic societal pressures. This shift can lead to improved emotional well-being and a healthier self-esteem.

5 **Innovation and Creativity:** Societal expectations can stifle creativity and innovation by fostering a fear of failure

and a reluctance to challenge established norms.

Individuals may prioritize meeting societal expectations over exploring novel ideas, limiting the potential for groundbreaking innovation. A culture that values conformity over creativity impedes the diversity of thought necessary for fostering new solutions and breakthroughs.

Breaking free from these expectations encourages unconventional thinking and fosters a climate where new ideas can flourish.

Innovation often arises when individuals are free to explore uncharted territories and challenge existing norms.

6 **Building Meaningful Connections:**

Authentic relationships are formed when individuals are true to themselves rather than conforming to societal expectations.

Genuine connections are forged when people embrace their true identity, values, and beliefs.

By avoiding conformity and expressing their authentic selves, individuals invite honesty and vulnerability into their relationships. This transparency fosters understanding and connection, as it allows for genuine interactions, mutual respect, and a shared appreciation for each other's true essence.

Breaking free allows for genuine connections with others who appreciate individuals for who they truly are, fostering deeper and more meaningful relationships.

7 **Cultural Progress and Social Change:** Societal progress often hinges on individuals challenging established norms.

Those who challenge norms drive change, fostering new ideas, perspectives, and solutions.

By challenging the familiar, individuals contribute to the evolution of society, pushing boundaries and fostering creativity. This process is essential for adapting to changing circumstances, addressing injustices, and ensuring that societies remain dynamic and responsive to the evolving needs of diverse populations.

Breaking free from social expectations contributes to cultural evolution and social change. Those who challenge outdated norms and push for inclusivity pave the way for a more diverse, accepting, and equitable society.

8 **Empowerment and Independence:** Breaking free from social expectations empowers individuals to take control of their lives and make decisions based on personal values rather than external pressures.

This sense of independence fosters empowerment, allowing individuals to shape their own destinies.

Breaking free from social expectations is a courageous journey that involves challenging ingrained norms and embracing one's authentic self. Here are some strategies to navigate this process:

1 **Self-Reflection:** Begin by reflecting on your values, passions, and aspirations. Understanding your true self is foundational to breaking free from societal expectations.

Consider what genuinely matters to you, separate from external influences, and identify areas where you have adopted beliefs or goals imposed by society.

2 **Clarify Your Values:** Clearly define your personal values and priorities. Knowing what truly matters to you allows you to align your actions and decisions with your authentic self.

This clarity serves as a compass, guiding you away from societal expectations that does not align with your core values.

3 **Set Personal Boundaries:** Establishing and communicating boundaries is crucial for maintaining your authenticity.

Learn to say no to activities or commitments that do not resonate with your values or contribute positively to your well-being. Setting boundaries helps create space for you to live on your terms, free from undue external pressures.

4 **Challenge Limiting Beliefs:** Examine and challenge any limiting beliefs or negative self-talk that have been ingrained by societal expectations.

Recognize that societal norms are not universal truths, and it's okay to question and redefine your beliefs based on your authentic experiences and perspectives.

5 **Surround Yourself with Supportive People:** Cultivate relationships with individuals who appreciate and support your true self.

Surrounding yourself with a supportive community can provide encouragement and validation as you navigate the path of breaking free from societal expectations.

Healthy relationships foster an environment where you can express your authentic self without fear of judgment.

6 **Embrace Imperfection:** Accept that perfection is an unrealistic standard often imposed by society. Embrace your imperfections and view them as unique qualities that contribute to your individuality. Recognizing and celebrating your flaws can be empowering and liberating.

7 **Cultivate Self-Compassion:** Be kind to yourself throughout this journey. Breaking free from societal expectations involve facing challenges and uncertainties.

Practice self-compassion by treating yourself with the same kindness and understanding that you would offer to a friend. Acknowledge that it's okay to evolve and redefine your path.

8 **Explore Your Passions:** Actively engage in activities and pursuits that bring you joy and fulfillment.

Rediscovering or exploring your passions allows you to connect with your authentic self and can lead to a more satisfying and purposeful life outside the constraints of societal expectations.

9 **Seek Professional Support:** If breaking free from societal expectations becomes overwhelming, consider seeking guidance from a therapist or counselor.

Professional support can provide valuable insights, coping strategies, and a safe space to explore your authentic self without judgment.

10 **Celebrate Your Achievements:** Celebrate each step you take towards breaking free from societal expectations.

Acknowledge your progress, no matter how small, and use it as motivation to continue forging your own path.

Embracing Self-Love and Acceptance

Embracing self-love and acceptance involves cultivating a deep sense of compassion and appreciation for oneself.

It begins with acknowledging and embracing one's unique qualities, both strengths and vulnerabilities, without judgment.

In a world that often emphasizes external validation, practicing self-love involves recognizing the inherent worth within, independent of external opinions or societal standards.

It requires a conscious effort to prioritize self-care and nurture a positive relationship with oneself. This process involves celebrating achievements, no matter how small, and learning from setbacks rather than dwelling on perceived shortcomings.

Here's why embracing self-love and acceptance is crucial in the pursuit of detachment:

1 **Reduction of External Validation:** When individuals cultivate self-love and acceptance, they become less dependent on external validation.

2 **Freedom from Comparison:** Embracing self-love involves recognizing and appreciating one's unique qualities and strengths. This self-appreciation diminishes the tendency to compare oneself to others.

3 **Release of Perfectionism:** Embracing imperfections and acknowledging that mistakes are a natural part of the human experience allows individuals to release the burden of unrealistic expectations. This self-compassionate approach contributes to a more balanced and

harmonious life.

4 **Improved Mental Well-Being:** Self-love and acceptance are integral components of positive mental health. Detaching from self-critical thoughts and embracing self-compassion leads to reduced stress, anxiety, and feelings of inadequacy. A more accepting attitude toward oneself fosters resilience and a healthier mental and emotional state.

5 **Enhanced Relationships:** When people genuinely accept and love themselves, they are better equipped to form connections based on mutual respect, understanding, and shared values. This, in turn, contributes to more fulfilling and sustainable relationships.

6 **Authentic Decision-Making:** Embracing self-love and acceptance empowers individuals to make decisions that align with their true selves rather than succumbing to external pressures or expectations.

7 **Cultivation of Mindfulness:** Self-love and acceptance contribute to mindfulness by fostering an understanding and appreciation of oneself in the present. This mindful awareness enables individuals to navigate life with greater clarity and intention.

8 **Strengthened Resilience:** Self-love and acceptance provide a solid foundation for resilience. Detachment from external

circumstances and setbacks becomes more achievable when individuals have a strong sense of self-worth and the belief that they can navigate challenges with grace and resilience.

Embracing self-love and acceptance through the art of detachment involves cultivating a healthy relationship with oneself while letting go of attachment to external validation and outcomes. Here are some key principles and practices to achieve this:

1 **Self-Awareness:** Begin by developing a deep understanding of yourself, including your strengths, weaknesses, values, and desires.

Regular self-reflection helps you become more aware of your thoughts, emotions, and behaviors.

2 **Mindfulness and Presence:** Practice mindfulness to stay present in the moment without judgment.

Detach from the past by letting go of regrets and detach from the future by releasing anxieties. Focus on the present and accept it without resistance.

3 **Acceptance of Imperfections:** Acknowledge and embrace your imperfections. Understand that perfection is unattainable, and everyone has flaws.

Practice self-compassion and treat yourself with kindness, especially during challenging times.

4 **Release Control:** Detach from the need to control every aspect of your life. Accept that uncertainty is a natural part of the human experience.

Focus on what you can control, such as your attitudes, behaviors, and responses.

5 **Letting Go of External Validation:** Stop seeking approval and validation from others to define your self-worth.

Understand that external opinions do not determine your value, and true fulfillment comes from within.

6 **Setting Healthy Boundaries:** Learn to say no to things that drain your energy or compromise your well-being.

Establish clear boundaries in relationships

to protect your emotional and mental space.

7 **Detachment from Material Possessions:** Recognize that material possessions do not define your identity or worth.

Detach from the pursuit of material success and focus on experiences and personal growth.

8 **Practice Gratitude:** Cultivate gratitude for the present moment and the positive aspects of your life.

Gratitude helps shift your focus from what is lacking to what is abundant and positive.

9 **Self-Care Rituals:** Engage in regular self-care activities that nourish your mind, body, and spirit.

Prioritize activities that bring joy, relaxation, and fulfillment.

10 **Positive Affirmations:** Use positive affirmations to reframe negative self-talk and reinforce self-love.

Affirmations can help shift your mindset towards self-acceptance and a positive self-image.

11 **Seeking Inner Fulfillment:** Shift your focus from external achievements to inner fulfillment and personal growth.

Identify and pursue activities that align with your passions and values.

The Liberation of Authenticity

The liberation that comes with authenticity is a profound and empowering experience, as it involves the courageous act of embracing and expressing one's true self without fear of judgment or societal expectations.

Authenticity liberates individuals from the constraints of conformity and the exhausting effort of maintaining a facade.

When people allow themselves to be genuine and true, they experience a sense of freedom that transcends societal norms and expectations.

Authenticity liberates individuals from the burden of living up to external standards and allows them to align with their internal values.

The courage to be authentic comes from a place of self-acceptance, where individuals embrace their strengths, weaknesses, and unique qualities. This liberation from the need for external validation fosters a deep sense of self-worth that is not contingent on others' opinions.

Furthermore, authenticity liberates individuals from the confines of superficial relationships. When people are true to themselves, they attract connections that resonate with their genuine nature.

Authenticity encourages openness and vulnerability, creating meaningful and fulfilling relationships based on mutual understanding and acceptance. This liberation from pretense and masks allows for more genuine connections, fostering a sense of belonging and originality in interpersonal dynamics.

Authenticity also liberates individuals from the internal conflict that arises when one suppresses their true identity. The liberation that comes with being authentic involves embracing one's thoughts, feelings, and desires without judgment.

This internal alignment brings about a sense of peace and harmony within oneself, contributing to overall well-being and mental health.

Moreover, the liberation of authenticity extends to the realm of personal and professional pursuits.

Authentic individuals are more likely to pursue paths that align with their passions and values, breaking free from societal expectations or external pressures. This liberation allows for greater fulfillment and a sense of purpose in life, as individuals follow paths that genuinely resonate with their authentic selves.

Chapter 6

Building Healthy Boundaries

Setting boundaries is akin to crafting a protective shield that preserves one's mental and emotional well-being while navigating the intricate dance of interpersonal relationships.

It involves recognizing and communicating personal limits, fostering a sense of self-respect, and acknowledging the importance of maintaining a healthy balance between connection and autonomy.

The art of detachment, in this context, is not about severing ties or isolating oneself but rather about establishing a discerning barrier that allows for meaningful connections without compromising individual integrity.

Building healthy boundaries is, in essence, an art form requiring self-awareness, clear communication, and a firm commitment to self-care.

It involves the recognition that everyone possesses unique needs, desires, and limits, and respecting these individual differences is fundamental to fostering harmonious relationships.

Establishing boundaries, within the art of detachment encourages individuals to cultivate a sense of inner strength and assertiveness, enabling them to express their needs and limits with confidence.

By developing these boundaries, individuals not only safeguard their own mental and emotional health but also contribute to the creation of mutually respectful and supportive connections with others.

Recognizing and Setting Personal Boundaries

Recognizing and setting personal boundaries is crucial for maintaining healthy relationships, both with oneself and others. Here are several reasons why it is important:

1 **Self-Respect:** Setting personal boundaries is a way of respecting oneself. It communicates to others that you have a sense of self-worth and are not willing to compromise on your values, needs, or well-being.

2 **Maintaining Emotional Well-being:** Boundaries help in safeguarding your emotional health. They prevent others from taking advantage of you emotionally, reducing the likelihood of stress, anxiety, or burnout.

3 **Healthy Relationships:** Establishing boundaries is essential for fostering healthy relationships. It creates a clear understanding of expectations and limits, preventing misunderstandings and

potential conflicts.

4 **Autonomy and Independence:** Personal boundaries allow individuals to maintain a sense of autonomy and independence. It ensures that each person can pursue their own goals and interests without feeling overwhelmed or controlled by others.

5 **Effective Communication:** Clearly defined boundaries facilitate effective communication. They enable individuals to express their needs, desires, and limits, leading to better understanding and cooperation in relationships.

6 **Empowerment:** Recognizing and setting boundaries empowers individuals to take control of their lives.

It encourages self-advocacy and the ability to make decisions that align with one's values and priorities.

7 **Preventing Resentment:** Without boundaries, there is a risk of building up resentment towards others.

Setting limits helps in preventing situations where one might feel taken advantage of or obligated beyond their comfort level.

8 **Balancing Priorities:** Personal boundaries aid in balancing different aspects of life, such as work, relationships, and personal time. They assist in prioritizing what matters most and allocating time and energy accordingly.

9 **Learning to Say No:** Setting boundaries involves learning to say no when necessary. This skill is vital for avoiding over-commitment and ensuring that one's resources are used wisely.

10 **Promoting Self-Care:** Boundaries contribute to self-care by allowing individuals to allocate time for rest, relaxation, and activities that promote their overall well-being. This, in turn, contributes to better physical and mental health.

Here are some key steps to recognize and set effective personal boundaries:

1 **Recognizing the Need for Boundaries:** Recognizing the need for boundaries is a crucial step in maintaining your well-

being and fostering healthy relationships. Here are some signs and strategies to help you recognize when you need to establish or adjust your personal boundaries:

Resentment and Frustration: Feeling consistently resentful or frustrated may indicate that your boundaries are being violated.

Reflect on situations that trigger these emotions and identify the specific boundary issues.

Overwhelmed or Stressed: If you constantly feel overwhelmed or stressed, it could be a sign that you are taking on too much or not setting limits.

Assess your commitments and responsibilities to identify areas where you need to establish boundaries.

Anxiety or Discomfort: Pay attention to feelings of anxiety or discomfort in certain situations or relationships.

These emotions can be signals that your boundaries are not being respected or need clarification.

Guilt or Obligation: Feeling guilty or obligated to meet others' expectations, even at the expense of your well-being, suggests a lack of clear boundaries.

Assess whether you are putting others' needs consistently above your own.

Exhaustion or Burnout: If you find yourself constantly exhausted or experiencing burnout, it may be an indicator that you are not setting boundaries around your time, energy, or personal space.

Physical Health Issues: Chronic health issues or exacerbation of existing conditions can sometimes be linked to stress resulting from boundary violations.

Pay attention to how your physical health is affected by your emotional and relational boundaries.

People-Pleasing Behavior: Constantly seeking approval or trying to please others at the expense of your own needs may indicate weak or nonexistent boundaries.

Assess whether you are compromising your authenticity to meet others' expectations.

Inability to Say No: Difficulty saying no or setting limits on your time and resources is a clear sign that you need to establish firmer boundaries. This can lead to over-commitment and burnout.

Unhealthy Relationship Dynamics: If you find yourself in relationships where there is a lack of respect for your autonomy, or if you feel controlled or manipulated, it may be an indication that you need to establish clearer boundaries.

Recurring Conflict: Ongoing conflict in your relationships may stem from boundary issues. Identify patterns of disagreement or tension and consider whether clearer communication and boundary setting could alleviate the conflict.

2 **Setting Personal Boundaries:** Setting personal boundaries is essential for maintaining healthy relationships, promoting self-respect, and safeguarding your well-being.

Here are steps to help you effectively set and communicate personal boundaries:

Self-Awareness: Reflect on your values, needs, and priorities. Understand what is important to you and identify situations where you feel uncomfortable or stressed. Self-awareness is the foundation for setting meaningful boundaries.

Identify Your Limits: Clearly define the limits of what you're comfortable with, whether they involve your time, emotions, personal space, or relationships. Knowing your limits is crucial for communicating them effectively.

Communicate Clearly: Use clear and assertive communication when expressing your boundaries.

Be direct and specific, avoiding ambiguity. Use "I" statements to express your feelings and needs without blaming others.

Be Firm and Respectful: Firmly assert your boundaries while maintaining respect for others' perspectives. It's important to strike a balance between being assertive about your needs and understanding the feelings of those around you.

Prioritize Self-Care: Understand that setting boundaries is an act of self-care. Prioritize your well-being and recognize that it's okay to put yourself first in certain situations.

Learn to Say No: Practice saying no when necessary. It's crucial to recognize your limits and be willing to decline requests or commitments that may compromise your well-being or values.

Be Specific: Clearly articulate the boundaries you are setting. Vague or ambiguous boundaries can lead to confusion and misunderstandings. Specify what behaviors are acceptable and unacceptable.

Consistency is Key: Consistently enforce your boundaries. This helps establish a pattern of behavior, making it clear to others what is acceptable and what is not. Consistency reinforces the importance of your boundaries.

Adjust as Needed: Be open to adjusting your boundaries as circumstances change. Regularly reassess your needs and be willing to communicate changes to those affected.

Seek Support: Share your boundaries with trusted friends, family, or colleagues. Having a support system can help reinforce your commitment to maintaining boundaries, and these individuals can provide guidance and encouragement.

Address Violations Promptly: If someone violates your boundaries, address the issue promptly. Clearly communicate the impact of their actions on you, express your feelings, and reinforce the importance of respecting your boundaries.

Use Non-Verbal Cues: Pay attention to non-verbal cues, such as body language, to reinforce your boundaries. Non-verbal communication can be a powerful way to convey your comfort or discomfort in a situation.

Evaluate and Adjust Relationships: Assess the impact of your boundaries on your relationships. Healthy relationships will adapt and respect your boundaries, while toxic ones may resist change. Be prepared to reevaluate and, if necessary, distance yourself from unhealthy dynamics.

Set Boundaries Early: It's often easier to set boundaries early in a relationship or situation. Establishing expectations from the beginning helps create a foundation of respect.

3 **Handling Boundary Violations:** Handling boundary violations is a crucial skill for maintaining healthy relationships and

preserving your well-being.

When someone crosses your boundaries, it's important to address the issue assertively and establish clear expectations. Here are steps to effectively handle boundary violations:

Recognize the Violation: Be aware of your own feelings and emotions. Acknowledge when a boundary has been crossed, and take the time to understand why it has affected you.

Stay Calm and Centered: Before addressing the issue, take a moment to calm yourself. Responding in a calm and collected manner will help you communicate more effectively.

Clarify Your Boundaries: Clearly communicate your boundaries. Use "I" statements to express how the violation impacted you and what specific behavior crossed the line. Be specific and concise.

Express Your Feelings: Share your feelings about the violation. Use assertive communication to express your emotions without blaming or attacking the other person.

Be Direct: Be straightforward in addressing the issue. Clearly state that a boundary has been crossed and explain why it is important to you.

Set Consequences: Clearly communicate the consequences of future boundary violations. This helps establish accountability and reinforces the importance of respecting your boundaries.

Use Non-Verbal Cues: Pay attention to your body language and non-verbal cues. Maintaining strong and confident body language can support the assertiveness of your verbal communication.

Seek Understanding: Encourage a dialogue by asking for the other person's perspective. Seek to understand whether the violation was unintentional or if there was a misunderstanding.

Establish Boundaries Firmly: Reinforce your commitment to your boundaries. Clearly state that you expect your boundaries to be respected moving forward.

Enforce Consequences if Necessary: If the boundary violation continues, be prepared to enforce the consequences you communicated. This might involve distancing yourself from the person or taking other appropriate action.

Seek Support: Talk to friends, family, or a therapist about the boundary violation. Discussing your feelings and seeking support can provide valuable insights and help you process the experience.

Assess the Relationship: Evaluate the overall health of the relationship. If boundary violations are frequent and the person consistently disrespects your limits, consider the long-term impact on your well-being.

Reevaluate and Adjust Boundaries: If necessary, reevaluate your boundaries and make adjustments. Sometimes, a violation can serve as a learning experience, prompting you to clarify or reinforce your boundaries.

Limit or End the Relationship: In extreme cases where repeated boundary violations occur, and the person shows little regard for your limits, it may be necessary to limit contact or end the relationship for your own well-being.

Self-Care: Prioritize self-care after handling a boundary violation. Engage in activities that bring you comfort and relaxation to help restore your emotional well-being.

4 **Saying No with Grace:** Saying no with grace is a crucial skill within boundary setting. It involves setting boundaries, prioritizing self-care, and maintaining a sense of autonomy. We'll discuss more about this later in the chapter.

Respecting Personal Limits

Respecting personal limits is an essential aspect of fostering healthy relationships and maintaining individual well-being.

At its core, this concept involves acknowledging and honoring the boundaries set by oneself and others in various aspects of life, such as emotional, physical, and time-related boundaries.

It reflects a profound understanding that each person has unique needs, comfort levels, and capacities, and respecting these limits is fundamental to creating a supportive and inclusive environment.

In interpersonal dynamics, respecting personal limits cultivates trust and builds stronger connections.

It involves recognizing when to give space, understanding when not to press for information, and appreciating the importance of consent in all interactions. This practice promotes a culture of empathy and consideration, as individuals actively listen to one another and respond with sensitivity to the diverse boundaries that define personal comfort zones.

By valuing personal limits, both in ourselves and in others, we contribute to the creation of environments where individuals can thrive emotionally and socially, fostering a sense of mutual respect and understanding.

Here are some steps to help you and others respect personal limits:

1 **Understand your own limits:** Reflect on your emotional, physical, and mental boundaries. Identify situations or behaviors that make you uncomfortable or stressed.

2 **Open and honest communication:** Clearly express your boundaries and limits to

others. Use "I" statements to avoid sounding accusatory, such as "I feel uncomfortable when..." or "I need some space because..."

3 **Active listening:** Pay attention to others' boundaries and be receptive to their needs. Encourage open communication and create a safe space for sharing concerns.

4 **Establish boundaries:** Clearly define your limits and communicate them to others. This can include personal space, time commitments, and emotional boundaries.

5 **Be assertive:** Stand firm in enforcing your boundaries, and don't be afraid to say "no" when necessary. Assertiveness

helps prevent others from unintentionally crossing your limits.

6 **Be observant:** Pay attention to verbal and non-verbal cues that indicate someone else's discomfort or need for space.

7 **Ask for consent:** Before engaging in activities or discussions that may push boundaries, seek permission and ensure everyone involved is comfortable.

8 **Understand situational factors:** Different situations may require different levels of flexibility with boundaries. Be mindful of the context and adjust your expectations accordingly.

9 **Respect cultural differences:** Recognize that individuals may have varying cultural backgrounds that influence their

perception of personal boundaries.

10 **Set aside time for yourself:** Ensure you have time to recharge and focus on your well-being. This may involve activities you enjoy or simply spending quiet time alone.

11 **Learn to say no:** Understand that it's okay to decline additional commitments when you feel overwhelmed. Prioritize your mental and physical health.

12 **Foster a culture of respect:** Encourage conversations about personal limits within your social circles and workplaces. Promote understanding and empathy for different needs and boundaries.

Saying "No" with Grace

Assertively saying "no" while maintaining grace is an essential communication skill that fosters healthy boundaries and mutual respect.

When declining a request or opportunity, it is crucial to express your decision with clarity and empathy. Start by acknowledging the request or invitation positively, showing appreciation for the consideration or thoughtfulness behind it.

Subsequently, diplomatically communicate your inability or lack of availability, providing a brief and honest explanation if necessary.

It is essential to convey your message with a tone of respect and understanding, ensuring the other person feels heard and valued despite your inability to fulfill their request.

Moreover, integrating grace into your refusal involves demonstrating empathy towards the other person's perspective and expressing gratitude for the opportunity.

Avoiding negative language or unnecessary apologies can help maintain a positive atmosphere during the conversation. Additionally, offering alternative solutions, if applicable, can showcase your willingness to contribute or assist in a different capacity.

By mastering the art of saying "no" with grace, you cultivate stronger relationships built on transparent communication, honesty, and mutual understanding.

Here are some steps you can follow:

1 **Pause and Assess:** Before responding, take a moment to assess your own feelings and the situation. Understand your reasons for saying no, and make sure you are clear about your boundaries.

2 **Be Clear and Direct:** When delivering your response, be clear and direct. Avoid ambiguous language that might be misinterpreted. Clearly state that you are unable to fulfill the request.

3 **Use "I" Statements:** Frame your response using "I" statements to convey that your decision is personal and not a reflection on the other person. For example, say,

"I'm sorry, but I can't commit to this right now."

4 **Express Gratitude:** Show appreciation for the opportunity or request. This helps soften the impact of the refusal and communicates that you value the relationship.

5 **Offer a Brief Explanation:** If appropriate, provide a brief explanation for your decision. However, be cautious not to over-explain, as this may give the impression that you're trying to justify your choice excessively.

6 **Maintain a Positive Tone:** Keep a positive and empathetic tone throughout the conversation. Emphasize that it's not a rejection of the person but a matter of

your current circumstances or priorities.

7 **Suggest Alternatives (If Possible):** If you can, offer alternatives or compromises. This shows that you are willing to contribute in some way, even if it's not in the exact manner initially requested.

8 **Stand Firm:** While being gracious, it's essential to stand firm on your decision. Don't be swayed by guilt or pressure. Reiterate your position if necessary.

9 **Practice Active Listening:** Pay attention to the other person's response. Acknowledge their feelings and concerns, and show that you understand their perspective.

10 **Follow Up:** After saying no, consider following up with the person to express

your continued appreciation for the relationship. This helps reinforce that your refusal was about the specific request and not about the person.

Remember, saying "no" is a skill that improves with practice. By approaching these conversations with empathy and respect, you can decline requests while maintaining positive connections with others.

Fostering Respectful Relationships

Fostering respectful relationships is a crucial aspect of building a healthy and harmonious society.

At its core, this concept emphasizes the cultivation of mutual regard, consideration, and understanding among individuals, whether in personal, professional, or community settings.

Respectful relationships involve acknowledging the dignity and worth of every person, embracing diversity, and actively listening to different perspectives.

By fostering an environment where individuals feel heard, valued, and understood, we lay the foundation for positive interactions that contribute to overall well-being and societal cohesion.

In practice, fostering respectful relationships requires intentional efforts to promote open communication, empathy, and conflict resolution skills.

It involves creating spaces where individuals can express themselves freely without fear of judgment, and where constructive dialogue becomes a cornerstone for resolving differences.

This approach not only enhances the quality of individual connections but also has broader implications for social cohesion, contributing to the development of inclusive communities that thrive on the principles of understanding, acceptance, and shared humanity.

Ultimately, the cultivation of respectful relationships serves as a powerful catalyst for building a more compassionate and interconnected world.

Here are some steps to promote and maintain respectful relationships:

1 **Active Listening:** Pay attention to what others are saying without interrupting. Demonstrate that you are engaged and genuinely interested in their perspective.

2 **Clear Expression:** Express your thoughts and feelings clearly, using "I" statements to avoid sounding accusatory. Be open to feedback and clarification.

3 **Empathy:** Put yourself in others' shoes to understand their feelings and perspectives. Show genuine concern for their well-being and validate their experiences.

4 **Open-Mindedness:** Be receptive to diverse opinions and ideas. Avoid making

assumptions or judgments before fully understanding another person's point of view.

5 **Respect for Differences:** Embrace diversity and appreciate the unique qualities of individuals. Recognize and respect cultural, religious, and personal differences.

6 **Establishing Boundaries:** Clearly communicate and respect personal boundaries. Understand and acknowledge when someone sets boundaries, and ensure that your actions are within those limits.

7 **Conflict Resolution:** Address conflicts in a constructive manner. Focus on the issue at hand rather than attacking the person.

Seek common ground and work together to find solutions.

8 **Promoting Equality:** Treat everyone with fairness and equality. Avoid favoritism and discriminatory behavior. Encourage an inclusive environment where everyone feels valued.

9 **Trust Building:** Foster trust by being reliable, consistent, and transparent. Keep your commitments and be accountable for your actions.

10 **Positive Feedback:** Acknowledge and appreciate others for their contributions and efforts. Positive reinforcement encourages a respectful and supportive atmosphere.

11 **Cultural Competence:** Develop an understanding of different cultures, backgrounds, and experiences. Educate yourself about cultural nuances and be mindful of how they may impact interactions.

12 **Self-Reflection:** Regularly reflect on your own behavior and attitudes. Be open to personal growth and strive to improve your communication and relationship skills.

13 **Conflict Prevention:** Proactively work towards preventing conflicts by fostering open communication, setting clear expectations, and addressing issues before they escalate.

14 **Promoting a Positive Environment:** Encourage a positive and inclusive atmosphere where individuals feel safe to express themselves. Create an environment that values collaboration and mutual support.

15 **Consistent Modeling:** Lead by example. Demonstrate respectful behavior in your interactions with others, and others are likely to follow suit.

Chapter 7

Embracing Change

Embracing change is a profound aspect of personal growth and resilience. It involves adopting a mindset that allows individuals to navigate the ebb and flow of life without clinging to fixed expectations or attachments.

Detachment in this context is not about indifference but rather a conscious choice to let go of rigid notions and embrace the fluidity of experience.

It requires a willingness to release the need for control and surrender to the transformative nature of change, understanding that every shift in life offers an opportunity for learning, adaptation, and ultimately, self-discovery.

The art of detachment in embracing change encourages individuals to view transitions as a natural and inevitable part of the human experience. By cultivating an open-minded approach, individuals can tap into their inherent capacity to adapt and evolve.

Detaching from the fear of the unknown and embracing change allows for a more profound connection with the present moment, fostering resilience and a deeper understanding of oneself. In this way, the art of detachment becomes a transformative practice, enabling individuals to navigate the currents of change with grace, flexibility, and a sense of empowerment, ultimately leading to a more fulfilling and enriched life journey.

Detachment from the Fear of Change

Embracing change as an inevitable and integral part of the human experience, individuals who cultivate detachment recognize that clinging to the familiar can hinder personal and professional growth. This mindset involves letting go of the paralyzing grip of fear, allowing individuals to approach change with a sense of curiosity, openness, and a willingness to learn.

In cultivating detachment, individuals liberate themselves from the shackles of resistance and anxiety that often accompany the unknown.

Instead of viewing change as a threat, they see it as an opportunity for self-discovery and improvement.

Detachment encourages a shift in perspective, enabling individuals to focus on the potential for positive outcomes and personal development that change can bring. By fostering this mindset, individuals not only navigate transitions more gracefully but also unlock their full potential to thrive in an ever-evolving world.

Here are some strategies to help you detach from the fear of change:

1 **Acceptance:** Acknowledge that change is a natural part of life. Embracing the idea that change is constant can help shift your perspective and reduce the fear associated with it.

2 **Mindfulness and Present Moment Awareness:** Practice mindfulness to stay present in the moment. Instead of dwelling on potential future uncertainties, focus on the here and now. Mindfulness techniques, such as meditation, can help you become more comfortable with the present moment.

3 **Reframe Your Thoughts:** Challenge negative thoughts about change by

reframing them in a more positive light. Instead of seeing change as a threat, view it as an opportunity for growth, learning, and new experiences.

Here are examples of reframing negative thoughts about change into more positive perspectives:

Negative Thought: "Change is scary and unsettling."

Reframed Thought: "Change may be challenging, but it also brings new opportunities for growth and self-discovery. Embracing change allows me to learn, adapt, and discover strengths I didn't know I had."

Negative Thought: "I don't like uncertainty; it makes me anxious."

Reframed Thought: "While uncertainty can be uncomfortable, it also means that there's room for exciting possibilities. It's a chance for me to develop resilience and become more adaptable in the face of the unknown."

Negative Thought: "I prefer the familiar; I don't want things to change."

Reframed Thought: "While the familiar provides comfort, change opens doors to new experiences and perspectives. It allows me to broaden my horizons, explore different aspects of life, and gain a richer understanding of the world."

Negative Thought: "I'm afraid of making mistakes during the change."

Reframed Thought: "Mistakes are a natural part of any learning process. Instead of fearing them, I can see them as valuable lessons that contribute to my personal and professional growth. Each mistake is an opportunity to refine my approach."

Negative Thought: "Change means leaving my comfort zone."

Reframed Thought: "Stepping out of my comfort zone may be intimidating, but it's where true growth occurs. Embracing change means pushing my boundaries and discovering capabilities and strengths I didn't realize I possessed."

4 **Set Realistic Expectations:** Understand that change often brings a mix of

challenges and opportunities. Setting realistic expectations can help you navigate the uncertainties without being overwhelmed by unrealistic fears.

Navigating uncertainties with realistic expectations can help you stay grounded and manage anxiety. Here are some examples of realistic expectations:

Change is Inevitable:

- Realistic Expectation: Acknowledge that change is a natural part of life, and unexpected events will occur.
- Unrealistic Fear: Believing that everything should stay the same forever, leading to anxiety when faced with change.

Adaptability is a Strength:

- Realistic Expectation: Understand that adaptability is a valuable skill, and you have the capacity to learn and grow from challenges.

- Unrealistic Fear: Fearing that you won't be able to cope with new situations, leading to a constant state of anxiety.

Imperfection is Normal:

- Realistic Expectation: Accept that nobody is perfect, and mistakes are a part of the learning process.

- Unrealistic Fear: Expecting perfection in yourself or others, which can lead to constant stress and disappointment.

Not Everything is Within Your Control:

- Realistic Expectation: Recognize that there are aspects of life beyond your control, and focus on what you can influence.

- Unrealistic Fear: Believing you should have control over every aspect of your life, leading to constant stress and frustration.

Failure is a Stepping Stone:

- Realistic Expectation: View failure as an opportunity to learn and improve, rather than as a sign of personal inadequacy.

- Unrealistic Fear: Fearing failure to the extent that it paralyzes you from taking risks or pursuing goals.

5 **Cultivate a Growth Mindset:** Adopt a growth mindset by seeing challenges as opportunities to learn and develop resilience. Embrace the belief that you can adapt and grow through change.

6 **Focus on What You Can Control:** Identify aspects of the change that you can control and those that you cannot. Direct your energy toward actionable steps you can take, rather than worrying about factors beyond your control.

7 **Create a Support System:** Surround yourself with supportive friends, family, or mentors who have experienced and embraced change. Learning from others' positive experiences can provide guidance and encouragement.

8 **Visualization Techniques:** Use visualization to imagine a positive outcome associated with the change. Visualizing success can help reduce anxiety and create a more positive mindset.

9 **Build Resilience:** Develop resilience by cultivating coping strategies that help you bounce back from challenges. This might include building a strong support network, practicing self-care, and developing problem-solving skills.

10 **Educate Yourself:** Knowledge can dispel fear. Educate yourself about the nature of the change you're facing. Understanding the reasons behind the change and its potential benefits can

make it less daunting.

11 **Take Small Steps:** Break down the change into smaller, more manageable steps. Tackling one aspect at a time can make the process less overwhelming and help you build confidence.

12 **Celebrate Past Changes:** Reflect on previous times when you successfully navigated change. Remind yourself of your ability to adapt and overcome challenges.

13 **Therapeutic Support:** If fear of change is significantly impacting your life, consider seeking therapeutic support. A counselor or therapist can provide tools and strategies to help you cope with and overcome this fear.

14 **Embrace a Learning Mindset:** See every change as an opportunity to learn and grow. The more you view change as a chance for personal development, the less intimidating it becomes.

15 **Affirmations:** Use positive affirmations to reinforce a mindset of adaptability and acceptance. Repeat affirmations that emphasize your ability to handle change with grace and resilience.

Adapting to Life's Unpredictability

Life is an intricate dance of unpredictability, a dynamic journey filled with twists and turns that often defy our expectations. The ability to adapt to life's unpredictable nature is a fundamental skill that not only defines our resilience but also shapes our personal growth and well-being.

Embracing the uncertainty inherent in life allows us to develop a flexible mindset, one that can navigate challenges with a sense of curiosity rather than fear.

Adapting to life's unpredictability involves cultivating resilience, the capacity to bounce back from setbacks, and the willingness to learn and evolve in the face of change. It requires a mindset that views challenges not as insurmountable obstacles, but as opportunities for self-discovery and growth.

In this ever-changing landscape, adaptability becomes a cornerstone for building a fulfilling and meaningful life. The ability to adjust to unforeseen circumstances fosters a sense of empowerment, enabling us to find creative solutions and seize new opportunities that may arise.

Embracing life's unpredictability is an ongoing process that involves letting go of rigid expectations and opening ourselves to the beauty of the unknown. It encourages a mindset that values the journey as much as the destination, recognizing that each twist and turn contributes to the rich tapestry of our experiences.

As we learn to adapt with grace and resilience, we not only navigate the uncertainties of life more effectively but also discover the strength within ourselves to thrive in the midst of unpredictability.

.Here are some strategies to stay adaptable through the art of detachment:

1 **Practice Mindfulness:** Engage in mindfulness practices, such as meditation or deep breathing, to stay present in the moment.

Mindfulness helps you detach from excessive worry about the past or future, allowing you to focus on what you can control in the present.

2 **Accept Impermanence:** Embrace the understanding that everything in life is impermanent. Recognize that situations, relationships, and even emotions are subject to change.

Accepting impermanence reduces resistance to the natural ebb and flow of life.

3 **Flexibility in Goals:** Be open to adjusting your goals as circumstances change. Detach from rigid expectations and be willing to modify your plans based on evolving situations. This flexibility allows for adaptation to unexpected turns of events.

4 **Cultivate a Growth Mindset:** Adopt a growth mindset by seeing challenges as opportunities for learning and growth. Detach from the idea that success or failure defines your worth, and instead focus on the journey and the lessons it provides.

5 **Letting Go of Control:** Acknowledge that not everything is within your control. Detach from the need to micromanage every aspect of your life and allow room for spontaneity. Trust that you can handle whatever comes your way.

6 **Focus on Process, Not Just Outcome:** Shift your focus from the end result to the process itself. Detach from being solely outcome-oriented and find fulfillment in the effort you put into your endeavors. This reduces anxiety about achieving specific outcomes.

7 **Learn from Setbacks:** Detach from the notion that setbacks are permanent failures. Instead, view them as temporary obstacles and opportunities to learn.

Extract lessons from challenges and apply them to future situations.

8 **Nurture Relationships without Expectations:** Approach relationships with openness and without rigid expectations. Detach from the idea that others must fulfill specific roles or meet certain criteria. Allow relationships to evolve naturally.

9 **Practice Non-Attachment to Material Possessions:** Detach from the idea that material possessions define your happiness or success. While enjoying what you have, recognize that possessions are transient, and true contentment comes from within.

10 **Embrace Uncertainty:** Detach from the need for certainty in every aspect of life. Life is inherently uncertain, and trying to control every detail can lead to stress and frustration. Embrace the unknown with curiosity and openness.

11 **Celebrate the Now:** Detach from the constant pursuit of future achievements. Celebrate and find joy in the present moment, appreciating the journey rather than fixating on an imagined destination.

12 **Seek Support and Perspective:** Detach from the idea that you must face challenges alone. Seek support from friends, family, or mentors. Others' perspectives can offer valuable insights and help you navigate uncertainties.

Finding Opportunity in Transitions

In the realm of personal and professional development, finding opportunity in transitions is a pivotal skill that empowers individuals to navigate change with resilience and adaptability.

Transitions, whether they be career shifts, life changes, or unexpected challenges, are inherent aspects of the human experience.

Rather than viewing transitions as disruptions, astute individuals recognize them as potential gateways to growth and transformation. Embracing change becomes an opportunity to reassess goals, acquire new skills, and cultivate a mindset that thrives amidst uncertainty.

The ability to find opportunity in transitions is not only a valuable personal trait but also a key competency in the business landscape.

In the dynamic world of commerce, companies that can proactively identify and leverage opportunities during transitions are better positioned for sustained success.

Whether prompted by technological advancements, market shifts, or global events, organizational transitions provide fertile ground for innovation, strategic pivots, and the cultivation of a resilient corporate culture.

By fostering a mindset that embraces change as a catalyst for progress, businesses can not only weather transitions but also emerge stronger and more adaptable in an ever-evolving landscape.

Here are some strategies to develop the habit of finding opportunity in transitions:

1 **Develop a Growth Mindset:** Embrace a growth mindset, where you view challenges as opportunities to learn and grow.

See transitions as a chance to acquire new skills, gain experience, and broaden your perspective. This mindset shift can help you approach transitions with a more positive and open attitude.

2 **Reflect on Past Transitions:** Consider previous transitions you've experienced

and identify the positive outcomes or opportunities that arose from those situations.

Reflecting on past experiences can provide insights into your resilience and ability to adapt, reinforcing the idea that transitions can lead to growth.

3 **Set Goals and Prioritize:** During transitions, set clear goals for what you want to achieve. Prioritize these goals based on your values and long-term aspirations.

Having a sense of direction can help you focus on the opportunities that align with your objectives.

4 **Maintain Flexibility:** Embrace flexibility and adaptability. Transitions often come

with uncertainty, and being open to change allows you to see opportunities that may not have been apparent initially. A flexible mindset enables you to adjust your goals and strategies as needed.

5 **Build a Support System:** Surround yourself with a supportive network of friends, family, mentors, or colleagues. Having a strong support system can provide encouragement, advice, and different perspectives during transitions, helping you identify opportunities and navigate challenges more effectively.

6 **Learn Continuously:** Use transitions as a time for continuous learning. Seek out new knowledge, skills, and experiences that align with your interests and goals.

This proactive approach not only enhances your capabilities but also opens up opportunities that may not have been evident before.

7 **Network and Connect:** Engage with others who have experienced similar transitions or who can provide insights and guidance.

Networking can lead to unexpected opportunities, whether in the form of collaborations, mentorship, or new career paths.

8 **Practice Resilience:** Resilience is the ability to bounce back from setbacks. View challenges as temporary and focus on building resilience during transitions.

This mindset can help you stay optimistic and see opportunities for improvement even in difficult circumstances.

9 **Celebrate Small Wins:** Acknowledge and celebrate small achievements and positive developments during transitions. Recognizing progress, no matter how small, can boost your confidence and motivation, reinforcing the idea that opportunities exist even in the midst of change.

10 **Cultivate a Positive Mindset:** Train yourself to see the positive aspects of transitions. Instead of dwelling on what might be lost, focus on what can be gained.

A positive mindset can attract opportunities and make the transition process more enjoyable.

Chapter 8

Mindful Productivity

Mindful productivity, is a deliberate and focused approach to accomplishing tasks while maintaining a sense of balance and mental clarity.

It involves the cultivation of a present-moment awareness that allows individuals to engage fully in their work without becoming overly attached to outcomes or overwhelmed by external pressures.

The art of detachment in mindful productivity encourages a harmonious integration of effort and ease, emphasizing the importance of staying connected to the task at hand while letting go of unnecessary stress and attachment to perfection.

In the pursuit of mindful productivity, individuals learn to detach from the incessant demands of multitasking and external expectations, honing in on the quality of their efforts rather than the quantity.

By fostering a heightened awareness of thoughts, emotions, and the environment, individuals can navigate their responsibilities with a more intentional and centered approach.

The art of detachment in this context becomes a tool for maintaining a healthy work-life balance, preventing burnout, and fostering a deeper connection to the intrinsic value of the tasks being undertaken.

Through mindful productivity, individuals not only enhance their efficiency but also cultivate a more profound sense of fulfillment and purpose in their endeavors.

Detaching from Busy-ness

In our fast-paced modern world, where the demands of work, technology, and social obligations often compete for our attention, detaching from the constant busyness has become a crucial aspect of maintaining mental well-being.

The incessant buzz of notifications, the pressure to multitask, and the perpetual pursuit of productivity contribute to stress and burnout. Detaching from this overwhelming busyness does not imply disengaging from responsibilities, but rather finding a healthy balance that allows for moments of stillness and reflection.

Creating intentional spaces for detaching from busy-ness is essential for mental clarity and overall life satisfaction. This could involve practicing mindfulness techniques, such as meditation or deep-breathing exercises, to anchor oneself in the present moment and break free from the constant stream of thoughts about tasks and deadlines.

Additionally, setting boundaries and establishing designated times for rest and leisure can contribute to a more balanced and fulfilling life.

By intentionally detaching from the hustle and bustle, individuals can foster a sense of inner calm, recharge their mental energy, and ultimately enhance their overall well-being.

Here are some strategies to help detach from busyness:

1 **Prioritize and Set Boundaries:** Identify your priorities and focus on what truly matters. Not everything is equally important, so set clear priorities for yourself.

Learn to say no when necessary. Setting boundaries is crucial to avoid taking on too much and becoming overwhelmed.

2 **Time Management:** Practice effective time management techniques. This includes creating to-do lists, setting realistic deadlines, and breaking tasks into manageable chunks.

Use productivity tools and techniques such as the Pomodoro Technique, time blocking, or the Eisenhower matrix to organize and manage your time efficiently.

3 **Mindfulness and Meditation:** Incorporate mindfulness practices into your daily routine. This could be meditation, deep breathing exercises, or mindful walking.

These practices can help you stay present, reduce stress, and gain a clearer perspective on your priorities.

4 **Unplug and Disconnect:** Take breaks from technology and social media. Constant connectivity can contribute to a sense of busyness and information overload.

Set specific times to check emails and messages, and consider implementing a digital detox by turning off notifications during certain periods.

5 **Delegate and Collaborate:** Recognize that you don't have to do everything yourself. Delegate tasks when possible and collaborate with others to share the workload.

Effective delegation not only lightens your load but also allows others to contribute their skills and strengths.

6 **Self-Care:** Prioritize self-care activities that rejuvenate your mind and body, such as regular exercise, adequate sleep, and healthy nutrition.

Make time for activities you enjoy, whether it's reading, spending time in nature, or engaging in hobbies. This helps create a balance between work and personal life.

7 **Reflect and Evaluate:** Regularly reflect on your goals and values. Ensure that your activities align with your long-term objectives and contribute to your overall well-being.

Periodically evaluate your commitments and responsibilities. Consider letting go of tasks or commitments that no longer serve your goals.

8 **Learn to Enjoy Downtime:** Embrace downtime without feeling guilty. Understand that taking breaks is essential for productivity and creativity. Use downtime to relax and recharge, whether it's a short walk, a coffee break, or a few minutes of quiet reflection.

9 **Develop a Healthy Relationship with Busyness:** Challenge the societal notion that being busy equates to success. Understand that productivity is not solely measured by the quantity of tasks but also by their quality and impact.

Cultivate a healthy relationship with busyness by finding a balance that allows for meaningful work and a fulfilling personal life.

10. **Seek Support and Communication:** Talk to friends, family, or colleagues about your feelings of busyness. Sharing your thoughts can provide valuable insights and support.

Collaborate with others to streamline processes and find more efficient ways of working.

Time Management Strategies for a Balanced Life

Effective time management strategies are crucial for achieving a balanced and fulfilling life.

In today's fast-paced world, individuals often find themselves juggling multiple responsibilities, including work, family, personal development, and social commitments. Without a thoughtful approach to managing one's time, it's easy to become overwhelmed, leading to stress, burnout, and a diminished sense of well-being.

Time management provides a framework for prioritizing tasks, setting realistic goals, and allocating resources efficiently, allowing individuals to navigate their daily lives with purpose and intention.

Moreover, implementing time management strategies contributes to the cultivation of a balanced and harmonious lifestyle. By organizing and structuring time effectively, individuals can create room for both professional and personal pursuits, fostering a sense of accomplishment and satisfaction in various aspects of life.

Balancing work and personal life, allocating time for self-care, and nurturing relationships become achievable goals when time is managed thoughtfully.

Ultimately, time management is not just about being productive; it's about creating a foundation for a well-rounded and fulfilling existence, where individuals can pursue their passions, nurture connections, and maintain a healthy work-life equilibrium.

Here are various strategies to help you effectively manage your time:

1 **Prioritize Tasks:** Identify and prioritize tasks based on their urgency and importance.

Use tools like the Eisenhower Matrix to categorize tasks into four quadrants: urgent and important, important but not urgent, urgent but not important, and neither urgent nor important.

2 **Set Clear Goals:** Define short-term and long-term goals to guide your activities.

Break down larger goals into smaller, more manageable tasks.

3 **Create a To-Do List:** Develop a daily or weekly to-do list to organize your tasks.

Update the list regularly, and celebrate achievements.

4 **Time Blocking:** Allocate specific blocks of time for different activities.

Schedule focused work periods with breaks in between to maintain productivity and prevent burnout.

5 **Batch Similar Tasks:** Group similar tasks together to minimize mental switching and improve efficiency. For example, respond to emails during specific time slots rather than throughout the day.

6 **Limit Multitasking:** Focus on one task at a time to enhance concentration and quality of work. Multitasking can lead to errors and decreased productivity.

7 **Use Technology Wisely:** Leverage productivity tools and apps to streamline tasks. Set reminders and notifications to stay on track.

8 **Learn to Say No:** Be selective about the commitments you take on. Saying no when necessary helps avoid overloading yourself and maintains balance.

9 **Regular Breaks and Self-Care:** Schedule regular breaks to recharge and prevent burnout. Prioritize self-care activities like exercise, meditation, or hobbies to maintain overall well-being.

10 **Reflect and Evaluate:** Regularly assess your time management strategies. Identify areas for improvement and adjust your approach accordingly.

11 **Learn from Mistakes:** Understand and learn from past time management mistakes. Use failures as opportunities for growth and refinement of your strategies.

12 **Establish Boundaries:** Set boundaries for work, personal life, and social commitments and clearly communicate these boundaries to others to maintain a healthy balance.

13 **Continuous Learning:** Stay open to new time management techniques. Attend workshops, read books, or take courses to enhance your skills.

14 **Celebrate Achievements:** Acknowledge and celebrate your accomplishments. Positive reinforcement boosts motivation

and encourages continued productivity.

Chapter 9

The Role of Gratitude

Gratitude is a transformative force that extends across various aspects of life, shaping perspectives and fostering a positive mindset.

At its core, gratitude involves a sincere acknowledgment and appreciation for the blessings, kindness, and positive aspects present in one's life.

It serves as a powerful tool within the realm of mental well-being, as practicing gratitude has been linked to improved mood, reduced stress levels, and an overall enhancement of psychological resilience.

In the broader context, gratitude extends beyond a mere expression of thanks and operates as a fundamental aspect of interpersonal relationships and societal well-being.

When individuals actively cultivate gratitude, they contribute to the creation of a more compassionate and empathetic community.

Beside this, acknowledging the positive contributions of others fosters a sense of interconnectedness and strengthens social bonds.

The role of gratitude, therefore, transcends individual well-being, playing a pivotal role in shaping a more harmonious and cooperative world by encouraging a focus on what is good, meaningful, and shared among individuals and communities.

Cultivating Gratitude as a Detachment Tool

Cultivating gratitude can be a powerful tool for fostering detachment, helping individuals navigate life's challenges with a sense of perspective and resilience.

By actively acknowledging and appreciating the positive aspects of one's life, individuals can shift their focus away from stressors and uncertainties. This intentional practice of gratitude encourages a mental and emotional detachment from negative thoughts and emotions, creating space for a more balanced and centered mindset.

Gratitude serves as a detaching force by promoting mindfulness and awareness of the present moment.

When individuals cultivate gratitude, they become attuned to the abundance of positive experiences, relationships, and opportunities surrounding them. This heightened awareness allows them to detach from excessive worry about the future or dwelling on past difficulties, fostering a mindset of acceptance and contentment.

In practicing gratitude, individuals develop a greater capacity to detach from the grip of negativity, enabling them to approach challenges with a clearer perspective and a more resilient spirit.

Here are some ways to cultivate gratitude as a detachment tool:

1 **Keep a Gratitude Journal:** Regularly write down things you are thankful for. This practice encourages you to reflect on the positive aspects of your life, promoting a mindset of abundance.

2 **Morning Gratitude Ritual:** Start your day by expressing gratitude for a few things. This sets a positive tone and helps you approach the day with a sense of appreciation.

3 **Mindful Appreciation:** Incorporate mindfulness into your gratitude practice. Take a moment to truly savor and

appreciate the experiences, people, or things you are grateful for. Mindfulness helps deepen your connection with the present moment.

4 **Express Gratitude Verbally:** Tell people that you appreciate them. Expressing gratitude to others not only strengthens your relationships but also reinforces a positive mindset.

5 **Detach from Material Possessions:** Detach from the idea that material possessions define your happiness. Express gratitude for the non-material aspects of life, such as relationships, health, and personal growth.

6 **Practice Acceptance:** Learn to accept situations as they are, without excessive

resistance or attachment to specific outcomes. Gratitude can help you appreciate the present moment rather than dwelling on what might be lacking.

7 **Gratitude Meditation:** Engage in gratitude meditation where you focus on being thankful for different aspects of your life. This can help calm your mind and detach from stress or worries.

8 **Limit Comparison:** Avoid comparing yourself to others. Cultivate gratitude for your unique journey and recognize the value in your own experiences and achievements.

Appreciating the Present Moment

In our fast-paced and hectic lives, it's easy to get caught up in the whirlwind of responsibilities, future plans, and past regrets. However, there is immense value in appreciating the present moment.

The present is a gift that unfolds before us, offering a unique opportunity to experience life in its raw and unfiltered form. By cultivating mindfulness and tuning into the current moment, we open ourselves to a world of sensations, emotions, and connections that might otherwise go unnoticed.

Appreciating the present moment is not about ignoring the past or neglecting the future; rather, it's a conscious choice to savor the richness of the now.

It involves slowing down, paying attention to our surroundings, and embracing the sensations that come with each passing moment.

The present is a canvas upon which our memories are painted, and by fully immersing ourselves in it, we can create a mosaic of meaningful experiences that contribute to a more fulfilling and well-lived life.

Moreover, the practice of appreciating the present moment has profound effects on our mental well-being. It reduces stress, anxiety, and the constant pressure of an uncertain future.

When we immerse ourselves in the current moment, we free our minds from the shackles of worry and regret. This mental liberation allows us to engage with life with greater clarity, creativity, and a sense of calm.

In essence, appreciating the present moment is not just a philosophical concept; it's a practical and transformative approach to living a more balanced and joyful life.

Here are some examples of everyday situations and ways to savor them:

1 **Morning Routine:** Instead of rushing through your morning routine, take a moment to appreciate the warmth of your shower, the aroma of your coffee, or the feel of sunlight on your face. Start

your day with a sense of gratitude for these simple pleasures.

2 **Mealtime:** Rather than eating on autopilot, savor each bite during meals. Pay attention to the flavors, textures, and aromas of your food. Take the time to enjoy the company of those you are sharing the meal with, fostering connection and appreciation.

3 **Nature Walk:** When walking outdoors, pay attention to the sights and sounds of nature around you. Notice the rustle of leaves, the colors of the sky, or the sensation of the ground beneath your feet. Connecting with nature in this way can be grounding and refreshing.

4 **Listening to Music:** Take a break from the hustle and bustle, put on your favorite music, and truly listen. Close your eyes, feel the rhythm, and let yourself be immersed in the melodies. Allow the music to evoke emotions and memories.

5 **Daily Commute:** Use your commute as an opportunity for mindfulness. Whether you're driving, walking, or using public transportation, pay attention to your surroundings. Take in the scenery, observe the people around you, and appreciate the journey itself.

6 **Sunset or Sunrise:** Pause to witness the beauty of a sunrise or sunset. Find a quiet spot, take a deep breath, and enjoy the changing colors of the sky. It's a simple

yet powerful way to connect with the natural world and reflect on the beauty of the moment.

7 **Reading a Book:** Rather than rushing through a book, immerse yourself in the story. Feel the texture of the pages, savor the words, and let your imagination create vivid images. Reading can be a relaxing and enjoyable escape into the present.

8 **Conversation with a Friend:** When engaging in conversation, be fully present. Put away distractions, make eye contact, and actively listen. Enjoy the exchange of ideas, emotions, and laughter. Meaningful connections with others can be a source of joy in everyday

moments.

9 **Gardening:** If you have a garden or even a small plant, spend some time tending to it. Feel the soil, observe the growth, and appreciate the beauty of nature. Gardening can be a therapeutic and rewarding activity.

10 **Quiet Moments Before Bed:** Take a few moments before bedtime to reflect on your day. Appreciate the small victories, express gratitude for positive experiences, and let go of any stress. Create a peaceful bedtime routine to transition into a restful night's sleep.

Shifting Perspective through Grateful Living

Shifting perspective through grateful living involves cultivating a mindset that focuses on appreciation for the positive aspects of life, even in the face of challenges. This transformative approach encourages individuals to actively recognize and express gratitude for the everyday blessings that may be easily overlooked.

By adopting a grateful mindset, people can shift their perspective from dwelling on what they lack or what went wrong to acknowledging and cherishing what they have, fostering a more positive and resilient outlook on life.

Grateful living invites individuals to

develop a heightened awareness of the present moment, encouraging mindfulness and a deeper connection with the experiences that shape their lives.

By consciously acknowledging and appreciating the small joys and positive aspects of daily existence, individuals can find solace and contentment amidst life's complexities. This practice not only enhances mental well-being but also strengthens emotional resilience, empowering individuals to navigate challenges with a more balanced and optimistic mindset.

Moreover, shifting perspective through grateful living extends beyond personal well-being to impact interpersonal relationships and community dynamics.

As individuals embrace gratitude as a guiding principle, they often become more compassionate, empathetic, and understanding towards others. This ripple effect can contribute to the creation of a more supportive and harmonious social environment, fostering a sense of collective gratitude that transcends individual experiences.

In essence, grateful living becomes a transformative force that not only shapes individual perspectives but also has the potential to positively influence the fabric of communities and societies.

Here are some ways to achieve this:

1 **Gratitude Journaling:** Write down things you're grateful for regularly, whether it's daily or weekly. This practice helps shift your focus from what's lacking to what's present and positive in your life.

2 **Mindfulness and Presence:** Be present in the moment and pay attention to the small things. Engage your senses in the present experience, allowing you to appreciate the details you might otherwise overlook.

3 **Reflect on Challenges:** Consider difficult situations as opportunities for growth. Reflect on what you've learned or how you've grown stronger through adversity. This reframes challenges as valuable

experiences.

4 **Express Gratitude:** Vocalize or write appreciation for others. It not only strengthens relationships but also enhances your own sense of gratitude.

5 **Visual Reminders:** Surround yourself with reminders of gratitude, whether it's a gratitude jar, sticky notes, or photos that remind you of positive experiences.

6 **Shift Focus from Wanting to Having:** Instead of focusing solely on what you want, recognize and appreciate what you already have. This shift in focus diminishes feelings of lack and amplifies feelings of abundance.

7 **Practice Compassion and Empathy:** Engage in acts of kindness and

compassion. This not only helps others but also enhances your sense of gratitude for the ability to make a positive impact.

8 Find Gratitude in Everyday Moments: Train yourself to appreciate the ordinary. Whether it's a sunset, a warm cup of tea, or a smile from a stranger, find gratitude in these small moments.

9 Shift Comparison to Celebration: Rather than comparing yourself to others, celebrate their successes and find inspiration in them. Recognize that everyone has their own unique journey.

10 Reflect on Past Blessings: Recall and acknowledge past blessings or moments of gratitude. Reminding yourself of these instances can reignite a sense of thankfulness in the present.

11 Cultivate an Attitude of Appreciation:
Make it a habit to appreciate the people, things, and experiences in your life regularly. This habitual mindset shift can significantly impact your perspective.

Chapter 10

Navigating Challenges

Embarking on a journey of detachment involves navigating a series of challenges that are integral to personal growth and well-being.

One of the primary challenges individuals face is overcoming the fear of uncertainty.

Detaching from the familiar can evoke feelings of vulnerability and discomfort, as it involves stepping into the unknown. However, it is in this space of uncertainty that resilience is cultivated, and the potential for self-discovery and adaptation becomes apparent.

Embracing the challenge of navigating uncertainty along the detachment journey empowers individuals to develop a greater sense of inner strength and flexibility.

Another challenge on the path of detachment is releasing the grip of past regrets and future anxieties.

Detaching from the burdens of the past and worries about the future requires a conscious effort to anchor oneself in the present moment.

Individuals may grapple with the tendency to ruminate over past mistakes or anxiously anticipate future challenges. However, through mindfulness and acceptance, one can learn to appreciate the current circumstances and approach challenges with a clearer perspective.

Navigating the challenges of letting go of the past and future projections is an essential aspect of the detachment journey, fostering a sense of liberation and a more profound connection with the unfolding present.

Overcoming Obstacles on the Detachment Journey

The journey of detachment is not always easy and may involve overcoming various obstacles. Here are some common challenges and strategies to overcome them:

1 **Fear of Loss**

Challenge: Detaching often involves letting go of the fear of losing things or people that are important to you.

Strategy: Develop an understanding that everything in life is temporary. Embrace impermanence and focus on appreciating the present moment without being overly attached to the future.

2 **Desire for Control**

Challenge: People struggle with the desire to control every aspect of their lives.

Strategy: Practice mindfulness and acceptance. Understand that not everything is within your control, and by letting go, you gain a sense of freedom and reduce unnecessary stress.

3 Emotional Attachment

Challenge: Detaching emotionally from people or situations can be difficult, especially when strong emotions are involved.

Strategy: Cultivate self-awareness and mindfulness. Recognize when strong emotions arise, and instead of suppressing them, acknowledge and observe them without getting consumed. This creates a space for rational decision-making.

4 Cultural and Social Pressures

Challenge: Societal norms and cultural expectations can influence attachment patterns.

Strategy: Reflect on your values and beliefs. Understand that societal expectations might not align with your personal growth and well-being. Choose a path that resonates with your authentic self.

5 **Misconception of Detachment as Apathy**

Challenge: Detachment is sometimes misunderstood as indifference or apathy.

Strategy: Clarify the concept of detachment for yourself. Understand that it's about maintaining a healthy distance from outcomes, not about being indifferent to people or situations. It allows for a more compassionate and objective perspective.

6 **Past Traumas**

Challenge: Previous experiences, especially those involving loss or betrayal, can make detachment challenging.

Strategy: Seek support through therapy or counseling to address past traumas. Healing from these experiences can make it easier to approach detachment with a healthier mindset.

7 **Immediate Gratification Mindset**

Challenge: Living in a society that often prioritizes instant gratification can make long-term detachment seem less appealing.

Strategy: Practice delayed gratification and set long-term goals. Understand that true fulfillment often comes from sustained effort and patience, rather than quick fixes.

8 Ego and Identity Attachment

Challenge: Detaching from one's ego and identity poses a profound challenge due to the deeply ingrained nature of these constructs within our psyche.

The ego, formed by societal influences, personal experiences, and self-perceptions, shapes our sense of self and defines how we interact with the world. Our identity, closely intertwined with the ego, forms the foundation of our beliefs, values, and behaviors.

Strategy: Explore practices such as meditation and self-reflection to gain a deeper understanding of your true self beyond external roles and identities.

Recognize that detachment from the ego leads to personal growth and inner freedom.

9 **Expectation Management**

Challenge: Detaching often requires managing expectations, which can be challenging when we have specific hopes for outcomes.

Strategy: Set realistic expectations and embrace the idea that outcomes may not always align with your desires.

Focus on the journey and personal growth rather than fixating on specific results.

10 **Social Relationships**

Challenge: Balancing detachment with meaningful connections can be tricky, especially in close relationships.

Strategy: Foster open communication within relationships. Share your journey of detachment with loved ones, allowing for mutual understanding. Encourage healthy boundaries that respect individual growth.

11 **Comparison and Envy**

Challenge: Detaching from the habit of comparing oneself to others and feeling envy can be difficult in a competitive society.

Strategy: Cultivate gratitude and self-compassion. Focus on your unique path and accomplishments rather than comparing them to others. Recognize that everyone's journey is different.

12 Resisting Change

Challenge: Detachment often involves embracing change, which can be uncomfortable for those resistant to it.

Strategy: Develop a flexible mindset and adaptability. Understand that change is a natural part of life, and by letting go of resistance, you open yourself up to new opportunities and personal growth.

13 Material Possessions

Challenge: Detaching from material possessions can be challenging in a consumer-driven culture.

Strategy: Practice minimalism and declutter your living space. Attach value to experiences and relationships rather than possessions. Shift your focus from accumulating things to cherishing moments.

14 Work and Career Detachment

Challenge: Detaching from work-related stress and defining self-worth through career achievements can be demanding.

Strategy: Establish a work-life balance. Recognize that your value extends beyond professional accomplishments. Engage in activities outside of work that bring joy and fulfillment.

15 **Overcoming Regret:**

Challenge: Detaching from past mistakes and regrets can be emotionally taxing.

Strategy: Embrace a growth mindset. Acknowledge past experiences as opportunities for learning and growth rather than dwelling on regrets. Use them as stepping stones toward personal development.

16 **Spiritual Detachment:**

Challenge: Detaching from a rigid interpretation of spiritual or religious beliefs can be complex.

Strategy: Explore a more flexible and inclusive approach to spirituality. Focus on the core values and principles that resonate with you, allowing room for personal interpretation and growth.

17 Balancing Detachment and Responsibility:

Challenge: Detaching might be misconstrued as neglecting responsibilities.

Strategy: Strike a balance between detachment and responsibility. Fulfill your duties with dedication but avoid being overly attached to outcomes. Recognize that you can exert effort without being emotionally entangled.

18 Mind-Chatter and Overthinking:

Challenge: Detaching from constant mental chatter and overthinking can be challenging.

Strategy: Incorporate mindfulness and meditation practices to quiet the mind. Focus on the present moment, allowing thoughts to come and go without getting entangled in them. This enhances mental clarity and reduces unnecessary stress.

Coping with Loss and Grief

Coping with loss and grief is a profound aspect of the human experience, and the art of detachment can play a crucial role in navigating these challenging emotions.

Detachment in this context doesn't imply emotional numbness or indifference but rather a healthy and balanced approach to processing grief. Here's how the art of detachment can be applied to cope with loss:

1 **Acceptance of Impermanence**

Detachment Principle: Recognize and accept the impermanence of life. Understand that everything, including relationships and experiences, is subject to change.

Application: When faced with loss, acknowledging the transient nature of life can provide a foundation for coping. This acceptance allows you to grieve without being consumed by the desire to cling to what has been lost.

2 **Observing Emotions Without Identification**

Detachment Principle: Detachment involves observing emotions without complete identification with them.

Application: When grieving, it's natural to experience a range of emotions, from sadness to anger. Practicing detachment involves allowing these emotions to flow without becoming overwhelmed by them. This observation can foster a more objective and mindful processing of grief.

3 **Bearing Witness to the Grieving Process**

Detachment Principle: Detachment encourages being present and bearing witness to the grieving process without being defined by it.

Application: Instead of getting entangled in the pain of loss, detach by observing your emotions and thoughts. This allows for a more measured response, facilitating the gradual healing process.

4 Finding Meaning Amidst Loss

Detachment Principle: Detachment involves recognizing that meaning and purpose can exist beyond the immediate circumstances.

Application: While grieving, seek meaning and purpose in the memories and experiences shared with the person or thing lost.

Detach from the idea that the loss defines the entirety of the relationship and look for positive aspects that contribute to personal growth.

5 Balancing Connection and Detachment

Detachment Principle: Detachment doesn't mean severing emotional connections but finding a healthy balance between connection and inner peace.

Application: Allow yourself to connect with the memories and emotions associated with the loss while maintaining a sense of inner peace. This balance prevents overwhelming grief from overshadowing your ability to navigate daily life.

6 Honoring the Process of Grieving

Detachment Principle: Detachment involves honoring the natural process of grieving without resisting or clinging to it.

Application: Allow yourself the necessary time and space to grieve. Detach from societal expectations or pressures to "move on" quickly. Honoring the process means recognizing that healing occurs at its own pace.

7 **Detaching from Guilt and Regret**

Detachment Principle: Detach from feelings of guilt or regret associated with the loss.

Application: Grieving often involves reflecting on the past, and it's common to experience guilt or regret.

Detach from these emotions by acknowledging that everyone is imperfect, and focus on learning and growing from the experiences.

8 Embracing Support Without Dependency

Detachment Principle: Detachment involves seeking support without becoming overly dependent on others for emotional well-being.

Application: While seeking support from friends, family, or professionals is crucial during grief, practice detachment by understanding that your ultimate healing comes from within. Use external support as a complement to your internal strength.

9 **Cultivating Resilience:**

Detachment Principle: Detachment fosters resilience by preventing overwhelming emotions from paralyzing personal growth.

Application: Cultivate resilience by facing grief with a detached mindset. This involves acknowledging the pain while maintaining a belief in your ability to adapt and grow through the process.

10 **Transcending Identity Attachments**

Detachment Principle: Detachment involves recognizing that your identity extends beyond the roles and relationships affected by the loss.

Application: Instead of defining yourself solely through the lost relationship, detach by acknowledging the multifaceted nature of your identity. Explore other aspects of yourself that contribute to resilience and strength.

Resilience in the Face of Adversity

Resilience in the face of adversity is a fundamental human quality that encompasses the ability to bounce back and adapt positively in challenging circumstances.

It is a dynamic and multifaceted trait that involves emotional, mental, and even physical fortitude when confronted with difficulties.

Resilient individuals exhibit a remarkable capacity to navigate adversity without succumbing to despair, demonstrating an innate ability to learn from setbacks, grow stronger, and emerge more resourceful.

In times of hardship, resilient individuals often display a positive mindset, viewing challenges as opportunities for personal and professional development. Their adaptive nature allows them to cultivate coping mechanisms, seek support from their social networks, and leverage their own inner strength to overcome obstacles.

Resilience is not merely about withstanding adversity but also about the process of transformation that occurs as individuals confront and overcome challenges.

It serves as a crucial asset in fostering mental well-being, fostering a sense of empowerment, and contributing to the overall ability to lead a fulfilling and purposeful life despite the inevitable trials that may arise.

Here's how the art of detachment contributes to resilience:

1 **Acceptance of Uncertainty:** When faced with adversity, those who practice detachment accept the unpredictable nature of life. They acknowledge that not everything can be controlled and focus on adapting to the present circumstances.

2 **Maintaining Emotional Balance:** Resilient individuals detach from extreme emotional reactions to adversity. Instead of being overwhelmed by fear or despair, they observe their emotions objectively, allowing for a more measured and effective response.

3 **Focus on the Present Moment:** Resilient individuals detach from ruminating on past failures or anxiously anticipating future challenges. They concentrate on the immediate actions they can take to address the adversity at hand.

4 **Flexibility and Adaptability:** Resilience often requires adapting to changing circumstances. Detached individuals are more open to adjusting their plans and

approaches, recognizing that holding onto preconceived notions can hinder progress.

5 **Learning from Setbacks:** Resilient individuals detach from seeing setbacks as personal failures. Instead, they view challenges as opportunities for growth and learning, extracting valuable lessons that contribute to future success.

6 **Cultivating a Growth Mindset:** Resilient individuals detach from fixed beliefs about their capabilities. They embrace challenges as a chance to develop new skills, deepen their understanding, and enhance their overall resilience.

7 **Seeking Solutions, Not Dwelling on Problems:** Resilient individuals detach

from the paralysis that can come with dwelling on the enormity of challenges. They channel their energy into identifying actionable steps and potential solutions to overcome adversity.

8 **Balancing Independence and Interdependence:** Resilient individuals know when to seek support from others and when to rely on their own strengths. They detach from the notion that asking for help is a sign of weakness, recognizing it as a strategic move toward overcoming adversity.

9 **Cultivating Inner Strength:** Resilient individuals detach from relying solely on external validation or favorable conditions. They cultivate inner strength

by drawing from their values, purpose, and self-belief, allowing them to weather adversity with greater fortitude.

10 **Appreciating the Transience of Adversity:** Resilient individuals detach from the idea that adversity is a permanent state. They appreciate that challenges, no matter how difficult, are temporary and that resilience lies in navigating through them with patience and perseverance.

Chapter 11

Living a Detached and Fulfilling Life

Living a detached and fulfilling life is an artful balance between engagement with the world and maintaining an inner sense of tranquility.

It encompasses the deliberate cultivation of a mindset that allows individuals to participate fully in life's experiences while not becoming entangled in the web of attachments and expectations.

Detachment here is not synonymous with aloofness but signifies a conscious choice to navigate the complexities of existence with a sense of ease and wisdom.

By embracing the art of detachment, individuals can break free from the shackles of unnecessary worries, allowing space for a more profound connection to the present moment and a fuller appreciation of life's diverse facets.

In the pursuit of a detached and fulfilling life, individuals learn to release the grip of excessive desires, opinions, and anxieties, fostering a greater sense of inner peace.

This art involves letting go of the need for external validation and acknowledging the impermanence of various aspects of life.

By embracing detachment, individuals liberate themselves from the burden of relentless striving, finding contentment in the simple joys of existence and building resilience in the face of life's inevitable fluctuations.

Living a detached and fulfilling life thus becomes a transformative journey, marked by a profound acceptance of reality and an appreciation for the richness that unfolds when one engages with the world from a place of mindful detachment.

Integrating Detachment into Daily Practices

Integrating detachment into daily practices is essential for embodying "the art of detachment."

It involves incorporating mindful and intentional habits that promote a balanced, resilient, and fulfilled life. Here's how to integrate detachment into daily practices:

1 **Morning Mindfulness Routine:** Start the day with a mindfulness routine that includes practices such as meditation, deep breathing, or mindful stretching.

This sets a positive tone for the day and helps cultivate a detached mindset by bringing attention to the present moment.

2 **Gratitude Journaling:** Incorporate a daily gratitude journaling practice. Reflect on and write down three things you're grateful for each day.

This practice shifts focus towards positive aspects of life, fostering a sense of appreciation and detachment from negative thought patterns.

3 **Setting Intentions:** Begin each day by setting intentions for how you want to navigate challenges and opportunities.

Setting positive intentions helps guide your actions and responses, promoting a sense of purpose and detachment from external pressures.

Here are some examples of setting intentions:

Gratitude Intention: "Today, I intend to start and end my day by acknowledging three things I'm grateful for, no matter how small they may seem."

Mindfulness Intention: "My intention for today is to practice mindfulness in all my activities, taking moments to breathe and be fully present in the present task."

Productivity Intention: "I intend to create a to-do list and prioritize tasks to maximize productivity, focusing on completing the most important tasks first."

Kindness Intention: "My intention today is to spread kindness. I'll make an effort to compliment, assist, or do something nice for someone, even a stranger."

Learning Intention: "Today, I intend to learn something new. I'll dedicate time to reading, watching educational videos, or engaging in a new skill or hobby."

Wellness Intention: "My intention is to prioritize my well-being. I'll ensure I take breaks, eat nourishing meals, and engage in physical activity for my health."

Focus Intention: "Today, I intend to eliminate distractions. I'll set boundaries, limit social media, and create a conducive environment for deep work."

4 **Mindful Eating:** Practice mindful eating by paying full attention to the tastes, textures, and sensations of each bite.

This daily habit encourages being present during meals, fostering detachment from distractions and promoting a healthier relationship with food.

5 **Digital Detox Breaks:** Take regular breaks from digital devices to detach from

constant connectivity. Set specific times to check emails and messages, and designate periods for technology-free activities.

This practice helps create boundaries and reduces the stress associated with constant digital engagement.

6 **Mindful Walking:** Incorporate mindful walking into your daily routine. Whether it's a short stroll during a break or a longer walk in nature, focus on each step and the sensations of movement.

This practice enhances presence and detachment from unnecessary mental clutter.

7 **Setting Boundaries:** Establish clear boundaries around work, social

commitments, and personal time. Learn to say no when necessary and prioritize self-care.

Setting and maintaining boundaries is a practical way to integrate detachment into daily interactions and responsibilities.

8 **Reflection Before Sleep:** End the day with a reflective practice. Take a few minutes to review the day, acknowledge accomplishments, and identify areas for improvement without judgment.

This nightly reflection promotes self-awareness and detachment from perfectionism.

9 **Mindful Breathing Breaks:** Take short mindful breathing breaks throughout the

day.

Pause, take a few deep breaths, and bring your focus to the present moment. This practice can be integrated into various activities, serving as a quick reset for a more detached and centered mindset.

10 **Single-Tasking Practices:** Embrace single-tasking instead of multitasking. Focus on one task at a time, giving it your full attention. This practice enhances efficiency, reduces stress, and aligns with the art of detachment by emphasizing quality over quantity.

11 **Self-Compassion Breaks:** Practice self-compassion during challenging moments. Take a brief self-compassion break by acknowledging difficulties, expressing

kindness to yourself, and recognizing that imperfections are a part of the human experience. This practice promotes detachment from self-criticism.

12 **Mindful Communication:** Bring mindfulness to your communication. Practice active listening, be present in conversations, and respond with intention. This daily habit fosters more meaningful connections and encourages detachment from unnecessary conflicts or misunderstandings.

13 **Sensory Awareness Breaks:** Incorporate sensory awareness breaks into your day. Pause to notice the sights, sounds, and sensations around you. This practice anchors you in the present moment,

fostering detachment from stressors and promoting a sense of calm.

14 **Periodic Digital Declutter:** Schedule regular times to declutter your digital space.

Unsubscribe from unnecessary emails, organize digital files, and clean up your digital environment. This practice reduces digital overwhelm and aligns with the principles of detachment.

15 **Evening Unplugging Ritual:** Establish an evening unplugging ritual before bedtime.

Disconnect from electronic devices at least an hour before sleep, engage in calming activities, and create a peaceful bedtime routine. This practice supports quality sleep and detachment from the demands of the day.

Celebrating Small Wins on the Path to Happiness

In the pursuit of happiness, acknowledging and celebrating small wins along the way is a fundamental aspect that often goes overlooked.

The journey towards fulfillment and contentment is not a linear trajectory but rather a collection of moments, both big and small. Recognizing and appreciating these small victories serves as a powerful catalyst for cultivating a positive mindset and fostering a sense of accomplishment.

Whether it's overcoming a personal challenge, achieving a minor goal, or simply finding joy in small pleasures, each step forward contributes to a more fulfilling and satisfying life.

The significance of celebrating small wins lies in its ability to reshape our perspective on the path to happiness.

In a world often fixated on grand achievements, it's easy to underestimate the impact of incremental progress.

By embracing and commemorating the smaller victories, individuals create a more resilient and optimistic outlook. This shift in focus not only promotes a healthier mindset but also instills the motivation needed to persevere through challenges.

Rather than waiting for major milestones to experience joy, finding fulfillment in the everyday accomplishments becomes a habit that enhances overall well-being.

Moreover, the celebration of small wins fosters a positive feedback loop that propels individuals further along their journey to happiness.

When we take the time to acknowledge and revel in our achievements, no matter how modest they may seem, we reinforce a sense of competence and self-worth. This self-affirmation, in turn, fuels the motivation to tackle more significant challenges and pursue loftier aspirations.

By recognizing the value in each step of the journey, individuals not only enhance their overall happiness but also create a sustainable framework for continued growth and personal development.

Consider these steps to commemorate and appreciate small victories:

1 **Acknowledge the Achievement:** Start by recognizing the accomplishment. Take a moment to acknowledge what you've achieved, regardless of its size.

2 **Reflect on Progress:** Reflect on how this small win contributes to your larger goals. Consider how far you've come and the steps you've taken to reach this point.

3 **Reward Yourself:** Treat yourself in a way that feels rewarding. It could be something simple like indulging in your favorite snack, taking a short break, or doing an activity you enjoy.

4 **Share and Celebrate with Others:** Share your achievement with friends, family, or colleagues. Celebrating together can amplify the joy and reinforce the significance of your accomplishment.

5 **Keep a Success Journal:** Maintain a success journal or log where you document these small wins. Writing them down helps reinforce their importance and serves as a source of motivation during challenging times.

6 **Visual Reminders:** Create visual reminders of your achievements. It could be a checklist, a progress chart, or even sticky notes with affirmations or celebrations of your wins.

7 **Set Milestone Celebrations:** Establish milestones for your goals and plan celebrations for reaching them. These could be mini-celebrations like a dinner out, a movie night, or anything that feels special to you.

8 **Practice Gratitude:** Incorporate gratitude into your celebrations. Take a moment to be thankful for the progress made, the efforts put in, and the support received along the way.

9 **Use Affirmations:** Create affirmations around your wins. Repeating positive affirmations related to your achievement can reinforce the feeling of success and happiness. Here are some examples to inspire your own affirmations:

- **For Personal Growth:** "I am constantly evolving, and today's small win is a testament to my commitment to personal growth. I embrace each step forward with gratitude and enthusiasm."

- **Overcoming Challenges:** "In the face of challenges, I am resilient and resourceful. Today's triumph is evidence of my ability to overcome obstacles and thrive in the pursuit of my goals."

- **Professional Achievements:** "I am a capable and accomplished professional. Each small win at work adds value to my journey, and I confidently embrace the opportunities that come my way."

- **Health and Well-being:** "I prioritize my well-being, and today's achievement is a reflection of my dedication to a healthy lifestyle. I am grateful for the positive choices that contribute to my overall health."

- **Building Relationships:** "My connections with others are strengthened through shared successes. Today's win not only celebrates my achievements but also deepens the bonds I share with those around me."

- **Learning and Development:** "I am committed to continuous learning and improvement. Each small win is a step towards mastering new skills and expanding my knowledge, contributing to my personal and professional development."

- **Creativity and Innovation:** "My creative spirit knows no bounds. Today's success is a testament to my ability to think outside the box, innovate, and bring fresh ideas to life."

10 **Celebrate the Process, Not Just the Outcome:** Remember that celebrating

small wins isn't solely about reaching the end goal. It's about appreciating the journey, the effort, and the growth that comes with each step.

Sustaining a Detached Lifestyle in the Long Run

Sustaining a detached lifestyle in the long run involves consistently applying principles that promote emotional balance, resilience, and a healthy perspective on life. Here are some steps to help maintain a detached lifestyle in the long run:

1 **Practice mindfulness:** Regularly engage in activities that bring your attention to the present moment, such as meditation or deep breathing exercises. Mindfulness

helps you become aware of your thoughts and emotions without being overly attached to them.

2 **Define your values:** Clearly identify your core values and priorities. Understanding what truly matters to you allows you to focus your energy on meaningful pursuits and reduces attachment to superficial or fleeting aspects of life.

3 **Acknowledge change:** Recognize and accept the impermanence of life. Understand that circumstances, relationships, and emotions are fluid, and holding onto them too tightly can lead to unnecessary suffering. Embracing change fosters a more detached perspective.

4 **Establish personal boundaries:** Clearly define and communicate your boundaries in various aspects of life, including relationships and work. Having well-defined limits helps prevent over-involvement and maintains a healthy level of detachment.

5 **Let go of expectations:** Cultivate a mindset of non-attachment by releasing expectations about how things should be. This doesn't mean abandoning goals but rather being open to various outcomes and adapting to the reality of each situation.

6 **Invest in self-improvement:** Shift the focus from external factors to your personal growth and development.

When you invest in becoming the best version of yourself, you are less reliant on external circumstances for fulfillment.

7 **Express gratitude:** Regularly acknowledge and appreciate what you have in the present moment. Gratitude helps shift the focus from what's lacking to what's abundant, reducing the need for excessive attachment to external circumstances.

8 **Simplify possessions:** Declutter your living space and minimize material possessions. Detaching from materialism can lead to a more liberated and content existence, where your happiness isn't dependent on acquiring or owning more things.

9 **Develop emotional resilience:** Strengthen your ability to bounce back from challenges and setbacks. Resilience enables you to navigate difficulties without being unduly affected, contributing to a more detached and adaptive mindset.

10 **Surround yourself with similar values:** Build relationships with people who share a similar outlook on life. Connecting with like-minded individuals can provide support and reinforcement for sustaining a detached lifestyle.

Conclusion

Detachment isn't about severing ties or retreating from the world; it's about reclaiming our autonomy, fostering resilience, and nurturing our well-being in a world that constantly vies for our attention.

It's an ongoing practice—a daily choice to prioritize our mental clarity, emotional balance, and spiritual growth.

As you navigate the labyrinth of your hyperconnected existence, may this guide serve as a compass, offering moments of reflection and guidance amidst the hustle and bustle.

Embrace the power of detachment as a catalyst for transformation, allowing it to infuse your life with a newfound sense of freedom, presence, and authenticity.

Your journey towards happiness and fulfillment in this hyperconnected world is unique, and the art of detachment is your steadfast companion—a tool, a philosophy, and a sanctuary in the whirlwind of modernity.

Let it be your guiding light, empowering you to forge deeper connections, nurture your passions, and savor the beauty of each passing moment.

As you close this book, may its teachings linger in your heart, prompting you to explore the depths of detachment and happiness in your own life.

Remember, the art of detachment isn't a destination but a perpetual evolution—a gentle reminder to embrace life's ebb and flow while nurturing your inner peace.

Paint the canvas of your life with the strokes of detachment, creating a masterpiece that resonates with joy, purpose, and a profound sense of fulfillment.

Your journey towards happiness in this hyperconnected world begins now, with the mindful practice of detachment leading the way.